Workplace Discrimination Prevention Manual

Workplace Discrimination Prevention Manual

Tips for Executives, Managers, and Students to
Increase Productivity and Reduce Litigation

By

David A. Robinson, J.D.

Adjunct Professor and Practitioner-in-Residence
University of New Haven
West Haven, Connecticut

Archway Publishing books may be ordered through booksellers or by contacting:

Archway Publishing
1663 Liberty Drive
Bloomington, IN 47403
www.archwaypublishing.com
1-(888)-242-5904

ISBN: 978-1-4808-0052-6 (sc)
ISBN: 978-1-4808-0053-3 (e)

Library of Congress Control Number: 2013905900

Printed in the United States of America

Archway Publishing rev. date: 5/2/2013

Table of Contents

Preface

This year (2013) marks the fiftieth anniversary of Reverend Dr. Martin Luther King Jr.'s "I Have a Dream" speech, delivered August 28, 1963, in front of the Lincoln Memorial in Washington. Dr. King said, "I have a dream that my four little children will one day live in a nation where they will not be judged by the color of their skin but by the content of their character."

Has the day Dr. King dreamed about arrived? Is race discrimination a thing of the past? The holiday in Dr. King's honor, MLK Jr. Day, this year coincided with Inauguration Day (January 21, 2013). America's first African-American President, Barack Obama, was inaugurated for a second term in office that day. Does this mean that Dr. King's dream has been achieved? Are Americans color-blind, rather than color-judgmental, in 2013? *Should* Americans be color-blind in 2013? Would Dr. King *want* Americans to be color-blind in 2013?

The answer to these questions, I think, is not fully yes or fully no. I explain in the book the circumstances under which I think it is OK for an employer to take race and skin color into consideration, and I explain the circumstances under which it is not. I do so regarding other categories of discrimination (gender, national origin, age, religion, disability, sexual orientation), too. This book explains employment discrimination law in 2013 and offers some tips to prevent employment discrimination lawsuits.

Much has changed in America in the last fifty years. America is no longer a "black and white" society. Racial integration has produced many shades of skin color in between. In addition, America has many more Asians, Middle Easterners, and other people from around the world than America had in 1963. Women are a much larger portion of the American workforce than in 1963. So are people with disabilities. Gay and lesbian employees are more open about their sexuality today than in 1963. Many mandatory retirement policies that were legal in 1963 are illegal today. Thus, older workers are a larger share of the workforce today than they were in 1963.

The median age of the American worker has increased also because people are living longer today than in 1963.

Yet there are also many aspects of American life that have not changed. Driving a car, eating a meal, putting clothes on, flying on an airplane, playing tennis, having sex, sleeping—these things have changed little if at all. Human nature does not change.

Fifty years after Dr. King's speech is, I believe, a good time to assess our employment discrimination laws and how best to comply with them *today*. The best way to comply with them *today* and *in the future* is not necessarily the same as it was in the 1960s, 70s, and 80s.

I hope to write a new edition of this book each year. It is a short book and should not be difficult to update. But one thing has changed a lot since 1963: my age. I was 10 in 1963. I am 60 in 2013. My present plan is to write an updated edition each year for as long as I can. My plans could change, voluntarily or involuntarily, but that is my present plan. Enjoy the book.

David A. Robinson
West Haven, CT
April 2, 2013

Introduction

This book is about some of the more common types of illegal discrimination in the workplace and how to prevent them: race discrimination, ethnicity discrimination, sex (gender) discrimination, age discrimination, religion discrimination, disability discrimination, genetic information discrimination, pregnancy discrimination, and sexual harassment (pregnancy discrimination and sexual harassment are forms of sex discrimination). By **discrimination**, we mean treating an employee less favorably because of one or more of those factors. Sexual-orientation discrimination (discrimination against gays and lesbians), which is illegal in approximately seventeen states in the United States, will also be discussed. Hopefully, this book will help reduce the number of employment discrimination lawsuits and reduce the damages and lawyers fees in such lawsuits.

There are some other types of illegal discrimination in employment, such as discrimination against an employee because he tried to organize a union, or because he took time off for jury duty, or because he "blew the whistle" on the employer (complained that the employer is doing something illegal), or because he filed a workers' compensation claim, or because he filed a claim for overtime pay, or because of some other type of illegal discrimination, but this book does not address them. It would be very difficult to address *all* the types of illegal discrimination in a short book such as this. That is because most employment laws contain some of type of "discrimination" prohibition, and therefore, in my estimation, it would take far more than 95 pages (this book is 95 pages) to spell out and explain them all. I think it is fair to say, however, that a large percentage (whether the percentage is 50 percent, 60 percent, 70 percent, or some other percentage, I am not certain) of all lawsuits filed by employees against employers are discrimination lawsuits involving the categories of discrimination addressed in this book, and therefore if employers will prevent the types of discrimination addressed in this book, the number of lawsuits against employers will diminish greatly. A large percentage of "wrongful termination" lawsuits are discrimination lawsuits involving the categories of discrimination addressed in this book.

A good way to remember the categories of discrimination addressed in this book is by the acronym REGARDS (race, ethnicity, gender, age, religion, disability, and sexual orientation). The acronym REGARDS was used in a report entitled *Best Practices in Achieving Workforce Diversity*, published in 2000 by the U.S. Department of Commerce and then-Vice President Al Gore's National Partnership for Reinventing Government. These categories— race, ethnicity, gender, age, religion, disability, and sexual orientation—are, according to the report, the "primary dimensions of an individual." Whether they are *all* of the "primary dimensions" of an individual is debatable. For example, these categories do not include such dimensions as an individual's intelligence, height, or physical attractiveness. Also, the government (the federal government and some state governments) has added a new category of discrimination that is illegal and, one might say, involves a "primary dimension" of an individual: genetic information. It is now illegal for most employers to discriminate against an employee based on the employee's genetic information, genetic history, or family medical history. The genetic information/history category is still quite new and developing in 2013, so this book does not address it much. Genetic information discrimination is, in many ways, like ethnicity discrimination or ancestry discrimination: you are discriminating against an employee because of his family medical history or genetics. You are discriminating against him because of what his genetics are or what you *think* his genetics are.

I want to point out that according to most dictionaries, the word "discriminate," in and of itself, does not necessarily mean something illegal or bad. If someone has "discriminating taste," that is usually good, not bad. Thus, not all types of discrimination are illegal. If an employer has two job applicants, one of whom scored high on an intelligence test and the other of whom scored low on that intelligence test, and the employer decides, based on that comparison, to hire the applicant with the higher score, the employer is "discriminating" on the basis of intellect. But such discrimination is, except in some unusual circumstances, a valid, legally permissible way to decide between two job applicants (so long as the test is not racially biased). The University of Connecticut (UConn) basketball team consists entirely of tall people. Does that mean UConn "discriminates against" short people? A person's height is largely predetermined; there is little, if anything, he or she can do to increase it. Many people who are not tall work just as hard and have just as much character, integrity, and athletic ability (for their height) as the UConn basketball players. I think short people and tall people should have equal rights. Does that mean I think UConn, which is a state university and thus part of the state government, "discriminates against" short people and denies them "equal protection of the laws?" No, I don't. My point is simply this: Not all discrimination is illegal. Not all discrimination should be made illegal. In our American democratic system, the government decides what types of discrimination are legal and what types are illegal, based on what the majority of people want to be legal and illegal. This book discusses some of the illegal types of discrimination in the workplace.

Most employers would like to *completely eliminate* the possibility of getting sued by an employee for discrimination or sexual harassment. But it is difficult to completely eliminate that possibility. Even if an employer does not violate the discrimination laws or sexual harassment laws at all, and even if an employer carefully documents an employee's poor job performance and gives an employee whatever warning or warnings a lawyer or human resources manager recommends, there exists a possibility—and the possibility increases if the employer *terminates* the employee—that the employee will at least *accuse* the employer of violating the discrimination laws and sue the employer. Whether the possibility is one in five, one in fifty, one in five hundred, or some other possibility, it is difficult to say, but the possibility exists.

There are some procedural strategies that many lawyers advise employers to use to prevent, or reduce the impact of, employment discrimination lawsuits, such as warnings, progressive discipline, employment-at-will statements, critical-incident documentation (documenting an employee's mistakes and other incidents of poor job performance), severance agreements in which the employee releases his right to sue, employment practices liability insurance, and perhaps some other procedural strategies. I agree with many of these strategies, but I do not have space in this short book to discuss them. I am trying to write a short book that will help employers prevent or reduce the likelihood of an employment discrimination lawsuit. Many employers want to read a one hundred-page book on the topic, not a one thousand-page book on the topic. Furthermore, my advice about procedural strategies will often depend on the size, type, location (Connecticut, Massachusetts, or other state), and other particular circumstances of the employer, and therefore it is difficult to generalize about such strategies in a short book such as this. If you want an exhaustive discussion of all aspects of employment lawsuits and how to prevent them or reduce the likelihood of them, you'll have to find some other book. Also, you should talk to a lawyer to ascertain what the best strategy is for your particular company or organization.

One strategy for preventing or reducing the likelihood of an employment discrimination lawsuit—and this book focuses on this strategy—is to **prevent discrimination in the first place**. This book teaches employers how to prevent some of the more common types of illegal discrimination in the workplace and thereby, hopefully, prevent or reduce the impact or likelihood of a discrimination lawsuit.

Another strategy is this (it is possible that there is an occasional exception to this strategy, but offhand I can't think of one). If you terminate an employee (that is, fire, layoff, or other situation in which an employee involuntarily is terminated from employment with your company or organization), don't *lie* to the employee about *why* you are terminating the employee. This does not mean that you must tell an employee *all* the reasons you are terminating him. Maybe you should tell him *some* of the reasons. In any event, don't tell him a *lie*. You can be vague; you don't have to explain things in detail. But don't tell a *lie*. If you terminate an employee who is black, female, older, disabled, or in some other category of discrimination discussed in this book, and you *lie* to that employee about *why* you are terminating her, she can use that lie *against* you in an effort to prove that your *real* reason for firing her was her race, gender, age, disability, or other category of discrimination. A judge or jury might deem your lie to be a *pretext*—a lie you told in order to cover up your *real* reason for terminating the employee. A judge or jury might assume that your *real* reason for terminating the employee was that you don't like blacks, women, older workers, disabled workers, or whatever classification that employee is in.

Let me illustrate. Suppose you fire an older worker because you think he is not intelligent enough for the job. You have a very intelligent young job applicant that you want to replace the older worker with. In your termination meeting with the older worker you try to be nice and you say, "We're sorry, but we're downsizing, so we have to let you go." After you terminate the older worker, you hire the young job applicant to perform that job. The older worker might sue you for age discrimination and *have a pretty good case*. Why? Because you *lied to him*. You were *not* downsizing. You replaced him with a *new hire*. This lie can be used in an effort to prove that your *real* reason for terminating him was his age. Does the law require you to be blunt and say, "You're fired because you're not intelligent enough for the job"? No, you are not required to say that. But don't tell him a lie. You can say, "We're not satisfied with your job performance" (if that is true). You can say, "We need someone who will produce more" (if that is true). You can say, "We need someone who is better with computers and spreadsheets (if that is true). There are other things you can say (if they are true). You can be vague. You can be tactful. Maybe, depending on circumstances, you don't have to give any reason at all. But don't *lie*.

An employer should not lie to an employee about *any* adverse employment decision. Don't lie to an employee about why you are demoting him, cutting his pay, reducing his hours, transferring him to a less desirable location, laying him off, or making any other employment decision that will displease him. If he sues you, he can use the lie against you in an effort to prove that your *real* reason for taking such action was his race, sex, age, or other category of discrimination. If you don't wish to tell him the true reason, then think of some way to be tactful without lying.

Here is one more strategy every employer should have. Become familiar with the website of the U.S. Equal Employment Opportunity Commission (www.eeoc.gov) and the website of your state agency that has jurisdiction over claims of discrimination in your state. The EEOC website and the state agency websites can be very helpful when trying to understand employment discrimination law.

Overview of Employment Discrimination Law

Employment discrimination law is founded on the principle that each person has characteristics that 1) the person cannot change (or would have considerable difficulty changing), 2) do not affect the person's job performance, and 3) some employers dislike. These characteristics include race, ethnicity, gender, age, religion, disability, and, in approximately 17 of the 50 states, sexual orientation (the REGARDS categories mentioned on page 2). As I stated earlier, a large percentage (I'm not sure what the exact percentage is; I would guess it is somewhere between 50 percent and 70 percent) of lawsuits filed by employees against employers are lawsuits alleging discrimination based on one or more of these REGARDS categories (race, ethnicity, gender, age, religion, disability, sexual orientation, and genetics). A large percentage (again, I would guess somewhere between 50 percent and 70 percent) of "wrongful termination" suits—suits alleging that an employee was fired wrongfully, illegally, or unfairly—are discrimination suits based on one or more of these REGARDS categories. They allege that the employee's race, ethnicity (or color or national origin; those four terms, "race," "ethnicity," "color," and "national origin," are largely, though not entirely, interchangeable), gender, age, religion, disability, sexual orientation, genetics, or rejection of the employer's sexual harassment is what motivated the employer to terminate the employee.

There are other types of "wrongful termination" suits, such as "whistleblower" suits, "violation of public policy" suits, "breach-of-contract" suits, suits by employees who were fired for alleging the employer underpaid their overtime pay, and some other types of wrongful termination suits, but a large percentage (I would guess somewhere between 50 percent and 70 percent) of wrongful termination suits allege race, ethnicity, gender, age, religion, disability, genetics, or sexual orientation discrimination. That is because most employees, including the vast majority of employees who are not in unions and do not have written employment contracts with their employers, are employees "at will." They can be terminated at any time for any reason, except they cannot be terminated for an *illegal* reason. Race, ethnicity, gender, age, religion, disability, and genetics are *illegal* reasons, as are some of the other reasons (for example, firing an employee for trying to organize a union) just mentioned. So to win a wrongful termination suit, they *usually* (not *always*, but usually) have to allege and prove they were fired because of their race, ethnicity, gender, age, religion, disability, or genetics. In approximately 17 states (including Connecticut, where I live and practice law), that list of categories also includes sexual orientation.

Some people refer to race, ethnicity, gender, and the other categories of discrimination discussed in this book as "protected classifications." Some people refer to women, people of color, older workers, religious minorities, the disabled, gays, lesbians, and bisexuals as "protected classes." In this book, I prefer not to use the terms "protected classifications" and "protected classes." Those terms often lead to confusion. Those terms might lead one to believe that only women, people of color, people over 40 years of age, religious minorities, disabled people, gays, lesbians, and bisexuals can sue for employment discrimination. The truth of the matter is that if an employer is subject to the employment discrimination laws, as most employers are, *any* of the employer's employees can potentially sue for employment discrimination. A white, Christian, heterosexual male can sue for discrimination if an employer denies him a job *because of,* or *on account of,* the employee's being white, Christian, heterosexual, or male. It is illegal for the employer to discriminate against *any* employee on the basis of race, ethnicity, gender, age (in most states, if 40 or older; but in a few states, discrimination against any employee due to age is illegal, so long as they are old enough to legally be hired for the job), religion, disability (as to disability, see pages 52-59 below; disability discrimination law is somewhat more complex than race discrimination law and gender discrimination law), or genetics, and in approximately seventeen states it is also illegal to discriminate against an employee on the basis of sexual orientation.

Another potentially confusing aspect of the term "protected class" or "protected classification" is that some people think it means that the employee cannot be terminated. They think the employee is "protected" from being terminated. Suppose, for example, an employee is black. He is thus in a "protected class." Some people think his being in a "protected class" means he cannot be terminated. They are mistaken. It means he cannot be terminated if *race* is the *reason* (either the motivating reason or the stated reason) for the termination. Was the employer, either consciously or subconsciously, influenced by the employee's race? If a *white* employee's job performance had been exactly the same as the *black* employee's, would the employer have terminated the white employee? If the answer is no, the black employee has a valid race discrimination lawsuit. The employee is protected from *race discrimination.* How will the employee persuade the court (judge or jury) that race motivated the employer to terminate the employee? Here is a brief answer to that question.

Obviously, the judge or jury cannot literally "read the employer's mind." So, the law gives the employee basically three ways to prove to the judge or jury that race was a motivating factor in the employer's mind when the employer decided to terminate the employee. One way is if the employer made any derogatory comments about the employee's race. I discuss this in Chapter 5 (Prevent Discriminatory Language). Such comments are evidence from which a judge or jury might conclude that race was a motivating factor. The second way is if the employee can persuade the judge or jury that the employer's stated reason for terminating the employee (the reason the employer stated to the employee or to others, or to the judge or jury) was, or is, not the true reason the employer had in mind. I discussed this on pages 4-5. The third way is if the employee can prove that the employer treated white employees better than similarly-qualified black employees. This third way is called "disparate treatment." I discuss this in chapters 1, 2, and 4. There is also a fourth way, called "disparate impact" (unintentional discrimination), but in my experience there is a fine line between "disparate treatment" cases and "disparate impact" cases. The tips in this book are designed to help you prevent against disparate-impact discrimination and disparate-treatment discrimination.

It is possible there are some additional ways an employee can prove to the judge or jury that race was on the employer's mind, but the ways I just listed are the usual ways. Furthermore, this book is not intended to be a treatise on how employment discrimination lawsuits are litigated. This book is mainly about *preventing discrimination in the first place*. This book is analogous to a book on cancer prevention: It is about cancer *prevention*, not cancer *treatment*. It might have a few things to say about treatment, but it is mainly about prevention: prevention of discrimination in the workplace.

Keeping It Simple

Having just heard that there are a number of types of illegal discrimination in addition to the ones addressed in this book, and a number of ways an employee can try to prove discrimination in court, you, as an employer, might worry that employment law has become too complicated. You might worry that you have to become a lawyer, or you have to be on the phone with a lawyer every ten minutes, in order to manage employees legally. Here is my response. Law, like medicine, can be complicated, but a lot of it is common sense. One need not become a lawyer to manage employees in compliance with the law any more than one need become a doctor to raise a healthy family. You should have some knowledge of law and medicine, and you should have a good lawyer or doctor you call for advice from time to time, but you can handle many day-to-day decisions yourself. This book tries to explain discrimination law in simple terms. This book tries to simplify, rather than complicate, your job as a manager.

How to Renew Your Library Items Online

This must be done <u>BEFORE</u> the due date.

1) Log in to **Connections**.

2) Under **Quick Links**, click "**Search for Library Materials at FSCJ.**"

3) In the top right corner, click "**My Account.**"

4) From there, you should see your loans and be able to renew them. ☺

JUN 1 3 2017   JUN 1 3 2017

"You" and "Your"

It is employ*ers*, more so than employ*ees*, who are required to comply with the discrimination laws. So when this book refers to "you" or "your," it generally means employ*ers*. However, employees can also benefit from following the advice. Furthermore, an executive, supervisor, or other manager can be simultaneously an employer *and* an employee.

Applicability

The rights of employers and employees depend in part on which of the 50 states they are in and how many employees the employer has. There are, to be sure, *federal* employment discrimination laws—which are the same in every state—but small employers (employers with fewer than fifteen employees) are not governed by most of those federal laws. Larger employers (those with fifteen or more employees) are governed by the federal employment discrimination laws *and* the *state* employment discrimination laws. Some states' employment discrimination laws provide greater protection to, and higher damage awards to, employees than the federal laws do. And many states' employment discrimination laws govern *small* employers (employers with fewer than fifteen employees) as well as larger employers.

So it is impossible for a book on employment discrimination law to give advice that applies to all employers in all states in all situations. Even advice as simple as "Don't discriminate on the basis of gender, age, or religion" does not apply to all employers. Small employers in some states have the right to discriminate on the basis of gender, age, and religion if they want to. Statements about federal law, such as "the most an employee can collect for emotional distress and punitive damages in an employment discrimination lawsuit filed pursuant to Title VII of the Civil Rights Act of 1964, as amended, against an employee with 20 employees is $50,000" have little or no significance in states such as Connecticut and Massachusetts, which have *state* laws that allow *higher* damage awards in employment discrimination lawsuits than the federal law does. The federal law is a *baseline*. Employers must comply with the federal law *and* comply with any additional requirements of state law. A simple example of this is the minimum wage laws. The federal minimum wage in March 2013 is $7.25 an hour. Does that mean that an employer in Connecticut is in compliance with the law if he pays an employee $7.25 an hour? No. The employer may be in compliance with the *federal* minimum wage law but the employer is violating the *state* (Connecticut) minimum wage law, which in March 2013 is $8.25 an hour (unless the employee, or the employee's occupation, is in a category that, according to the Connecticut wage law, can be paid less than $8.25 an hour).

That is why this is a short book. Very little can be said that is true for all employers in all states. This book tries to be applicable to as many employers as possible, but there may be occasional exceptions to its contents, depending on which state the employer is in and other unique circumstances of the particular employer. The book cannot address *all* the possible exceptions. That is why, if you need legal advice about a particular situation, you should consult a lawyer in your state.

Chapter One

Prevent Race Discrimination

"Racial superiority is a mere pigment of the imagination."
Dr. Laurence J. Peter (author of *The Peter Principle*[1])

Be Color-Blind, Except in a Few Situations

Be color-blind. If that is impossible for you, then be as color-blind as possible. That is the lesson learned from the U.S. Supreme Court's 2009 decision in the case of *Ricci v. DeStephano*, which involved white New Haven, Conn., firefighters who sought to be promoted and who outscored black firefighters on a promotion exam but who, due to the city's desire to promote more black firefighters and achieve greater diversity, were not promoted. You should ignore race and skin color completely, except in two or three situations that will be discussed below. You should not even mention race or skin color in the workplace unless you really have to.

If you are a boss and you enjoy friendly, constructive, well-intentioned discussions about race and culture, that is wonderful, but try, if at all possible, to do it *outside* the workplace and with people who are *not* your employees.

---

[1] This quote is not from *The Peter Principle*, however; it is a quote from Dr. Peter's book *Peter's Quotations: Ideas for Our Time* (New York: Bantam, 1979), p. 441.

The book will have more to say about diversity training, affirmative action, and multiculturalism later in this chapter.

(This book uses the words *race* and *color* interchangeably. Although the two words occasionally have different meanings in the employment discrimination context, they usually have the same meaning. So when I say race, I also mean color, and when I say color, I also mean race. Most of what I say in this book about *race* and *color* also applies to *ethnicity, national origin,* and *ancestry.* There is considerable, though not total, overlap among those five words or terms.)

Some people don't want employers to be color-blind. They want employers to notice and think about race and color. Some of them want *reverse* discrimination: They want you to hire a less-qualified job applicant of a certain race over a more-qualified job applicant of another race just to achieve racial diversity and to correct any past discrimination. Or they say color-blindness is impossible. "As long as people have eyes, they won't be color-blind," they say.

They have good intentions. But *they* are not *the law. The law* generally requires you to be color-blind when dealing with your employees. Here is what the primary federal employment discrimination law, Title VII of the Civil Rights Act of 1964, says:

> It shall be an unlawful employment practice for an employer
> to fail or refuse to hire or to discharge any individual,
> or otherwise to discriminate against any individual with
> respect to his compensation, terms, conditions, or privileges
> of employment, because of such individual's race, color,
> religion, sex, or national origin; or to limit, segregate,
> or classify his employees or applicants for employment
> in any way which would deprive or tend to deprive any
> individual of employment opportunities or otherwise
> adversely affect his status as an employee, because of such
> individual's race, color, religion, sex, or national origin.[2]

---

2   42 U.S.C. § 2000e-2(a)(I) & (2). There are also federal laws pertaining to age discrimination, disability discrimination, and genetics discrimination. In legal terminology and in this book, "U.S.C." means United States Code, not University of Southern California. The United States Code is a compilation of federal statutes. The "§" symbol means "section." This statute is title 42 of the United States Code, section 2000e-2(a)(I) & (2).

There is another federal law that pertains exclusively to race discrimination and thus somewhat overlaps Title VII. This other federal law—the Civil Rights Act of 1866, as amended by the Civil Rights Act of 1991 (hereinafter CRA 1866)—pertains to the formation of contracts. The Supreme Court has held that for the purposes of CRA 1866, the employment relationship is a contract.[3] Therefore, CRA 1866 applies to employers. CRA 1866 says, "All persons . . .shall have the same right . . .to make and enforce contracts . . . as is enjoyed by white citizens."[4] That means that every citizen has the same employment rights that white citizens have. CRA 1866 applies to nearly all employers in the United States. That means that nearly all employers, even very small employers (or nearly all very small employers), in all states, are prohibited from discriminating against an employee on the basis of race or color. Being color-blind significantly reduces your risk of being sued for race discrimination.

The Reverend Dr. Martin Luther King, Jr.'s goal was a color-blind society. "I have a dream that my four little children will one day live in a nation where they will not be judged by the color of their skin but by the content of their character," he said in his "I Have a Dream" speech.

Whether color-blindness is a good way or bad way to address the problem of racial inequality in the U.S. is an important question but not a question that should be foremost in an employer's mind. The foremost question in an employer's mind should be, What does *the law* say? The law generally (again, there are occasional exceptions) says, in essence, exactly what Dr. King said: *Don't judge people by the color of their skin.* If you don't like the law, then you can, if you want, lobby to change the law. But until the law is changed, you should comply with existing law.

Today (2013) the U.S. is not a "black and white" society. It is a society in which it is harder and harder to tell whose ancestors were from where. It is harder and harder to classify people as "black" or "white." A person from India might have darker skin than an African American. In 1963, the person from India was in India. Today he is, or might be, in the United States. Does an employer hire "blacks" when the employer hires people from India? What if a person has an African parent and an Indian parent? Is the person "black?" What if a person has a Mexican parent and an Indian parent? What

---

3   *CBOCS West, Inc. v. Humphries*, 553 U.S. 442 (2008).

4   42 U.S.C. § 1981(a). Although this law dates back to 1866, it is still the law today, as amended by the Civil Rights Act of 1991.

race is that person? What if that person is now married to an Irish-American and they conceive children? What race or color are their children?

In America in 2013, fifty years after Dr. King's speech, the simplicity, if it ever was simple, of "black and white" is long gone. It is much more difficult to classify people today as "black" or "white." The more you think about race and skin color today, the more confused you will be. Obey the law. Be color-blind unless there is a very good, legally valid reason not to be color-blind. An example of a very good, legally valid reason not to be race-blind and color-blind is if a government agency such as the U.S. Equal Employment Opportunity Commission (EEOC) requires you to provide the government with statistics about the racial composition of your workforce. The EEOC requires some employers to do so. To the extent that you need to notice, rather than be "blind" to, the race and skin color of your employees to comply with that requirement, do so. Do what the government requires. Another example, often related to the first example, is to comply with a government-mandated affirmative action plan. In general, though, you should, as much as legally possible, treat everyone as though they are members of the same race: the human race.

To those who argue that it is impossible to be color-blind (that is, they argue that it is impossible to ignore the race and skin color of your employees), I recommend that employers at least *try* to be color-blind. Even if you don't fully succeed in being color-blind, you should at least *try* to be color-blind. The more color-blind you are when dealing with your employees, the less discrimination there will be and the fewer employment discrimination lawsuits there will be.

Some people think color-blindness means treating all people as though they are white. That is not what color-blindness means. Color-blindness means being uninfluenced by whatever race or color a person happens to be. It means being uninfluenced by light ("white") skin, uninfluenced by dark ("black") skin, and uninfluenced by every shade of skin in between. It means regarding all workers as belonging to one race: the human race.

Some people argue that color-blindness is a form of racism because, they argue, color-blindness fails to take into account the history of racism in the United States and the importance to many people of their race and skin color. To those who argue that color-blindness is a form of racism, I respond, "Then we are damned if we do and damned if we don't." If we take race into account when making personnel decisions, we violate the law. If we do *not* take race into account when making personnel decisions, we offend the people who believe that color-blindness is a form of racism.

You cannot please everybody. Your primary obligation is to *comply with the law*. In a democracy, the law reflects the will of the majority of the people. By being color-blind, you are pleasing the vast majority of Americans and you are complying with the law. Maybe you are not pleasing everybody, but it is impossible to please everybody. It is better to displease a few people than to violate the law and lose thousands of dollars in a discrimination lawsuit.

Furthermore, I am not urging *total* color-blindness. *Blindness* does not necessarily mean *total* lack of sight. A person can be *legally blind* yet still have *some* (limited) visual perception. This book acknowledges that there are a few possible exceptions to my suggestion to be color-blind (see Exceptions, pages 18-19 below; see also Summary, page 27 below).

How to Be Color-Blind

Here are some suggestions to help you become color-blind. They are mental exercises to help you rid yourself of racist thoughts (if you have any). If you have no racist thoughts, you can skip ahead to page 18.

But if you are one of those people who believe that some races are smarter or better than others, here are some suggestions.

First, always keep in mind this fact: *Skin color is just a sunscreen*. Skin color has nothing to do with brainpower. Dark skin means that a person's distant ancestors were from a part of the world where it is sunny and hot most of the time, such as Africa or other places near the Earth's Equator. Dark skin was nature's way of protecting them from the sun's rays. Light skin means one's distant ancestors were from colder, less-sunny climates such as Scandinavia, Ireland, England, Poland, and Russia, and did not need such sun protection. Always keep in mind the following superb analysis that appeared in a 1997 *New Haven Register* article about race:

> Homo sapiens [human beings] originated in Eastern Africa
> about 200,000 years ago. Then, about 100,000 years ago,
> a group of this original population of modern humans left
> Africa and spread out among the world.
> [A]ll early modern humans probably appeared similar
> to populations in Africa, and then adapted to the different

environments in which they settled.

"If you look at an ultraviolet map of the world,
it correlates with human skin color," said [Nicholas]
Bellantoni [then a University of Connecticut anthropology
professor, now the State Archeologist of Connecticut].

Skin with sun-blocking dark pigment is a significant
advantage to people in extremely sunny climates. However,
people who settled in Northern Europe received less benefit
from skin pigment, which they slowly lost.[5]

Skin color is thus a function of *climate*, not *brainpower*. Keep that in mind, and you will liberate yourself from prejudice.

Here are some more tips for employers. First, don't "accentuate the negative." One element of racist thinking is to notice the race of a person only when the person does something bad or stupid but not notice it when the person does something good or smart. If a black person lets a white person cut in line in front of him in stalled traffic, the white person appreciates that, but the fact that this good person is black does not always register in the white person's mind. However, if the black person had *not* let the white person cut in, the white person would most likely have noticed that the "inconsiderate" person is black. If a white person is given the correct change by ten consecutive black store clerks but the wrong change by the eleventh one, the white person might fixate on the eleventh one. It probably did not occur to this white person that three of the last ten *white* store clerks also gave him the wrong change.

Second, don't judge the intelligence of the black population by their scores on standardized tests in school. Blacks tend, on average, to score lower on SATs and IQ tests than whites and Asians do. Does that mean they are less intelligent than whites and Asians? No. Does it mean that schools in black neighborhoods are inferior to schools in white neighborhoods? Maybe some are, but many are not. What it really means is that blacks (not *all* blacks, but many blacks) don't like taking these

---

5   Abram Katz, "One Race," *New Haven Register*, Oct. 26, 1997, p. A8. For a more recent, detailed discussion of this topic, see Nina G. Jablonski & George Chaplin (2010), "Human Skin Pigmentation as an Adaptation to UV Radiation," *PNAS* (Proceedings of the National Academy of Sciences) *107*(2), 8962-8968; retrieved from http://www.pnas.org/content/107/suppl.2/8962.long (last visited Mar. 14, 2013).

tests.[6] Many blacks don't try their hardest on these tests. Why? Because they don't like being "tested" by whites, especially for no reason. Blacks enjoy school as much as whites and Asians do,[7] and learn as much in school as whites and Asians do. But blacks are more likely to differentiate "testing" from schooling. They don't like being tested just for the sake of being tested.[8] The purpose of an IQ test or SAT is not to educate but to . . . test! Many blacks find it demeaning to be "tested" or "ranked" in school, especially when the tests and rankings are administered by *whites*. Being oppressed is bad enough. Being "tested" or "ranked" by the oppressor is even worse.

Employment tests are different. They are for the purpose of *hiring*. They help determine whether someone will earn a living. They really count! Blacks

---

6   See "Equal Protection and Intelligence Classifications," 26 *Stanford Law Review* 647, 648 n.5 (1974) (to many blacks, IQ tests and aptitude tests "reflect the values and promote the goals of the white, middle-class establishment; their use is seen as antagonistic to the long-term interests of members of minority cultures").

7   Black students spend as much time on homework as white students do and have the same attendance rate as white students have. Philip J. Cook and Jens Ludwig, "The Burden of 'Acting White': Do Black Adolescents Disparage Academic Achievement?" in Christopher Jencks and Meredith Phillips, eds., *The Black-White Test Score Gap* (Washington, D.C.: Brookings Institution Press, 1998), p. 390 (hereinafter *The Black-White Test Score Gap*). For a more recent discussion, published by the organization (the Educational Testing Service, or ETS) that administers the SAT, see Paul E. Barton & Richard J. Coley, *The Black-White Achievement Gap: When Progress Stopped* (2010), retrieved from http://www.ets.org/Media/Research/pdf/PICBWGAP.pdf (last visited Mar. 14, 2013).

8   Black students tend to do more poorly on tests if they know that the sole purpose of the test is to measure their intelligence. Christopher Jencks, "Racial Bias in Testing," in *The Black-White Test Score Gap*, note 13 above, at p. 70. Blacks (and women) tend to distrust these tests because they believe that these tests have historically been used by white males to perpetuate white male dominance. *Id.* Blacks are more likely to think these tests are "tricky and unfair" than whites are. Claude M. Steele and Joshua Aronson, "Stereotype Threat and the Test Performance of Academically Successful African Americans," in *The Black-White Test Score Gap*, p. 417. This causes them discomfit not only during the test but the night before the test, so they do not sleep well the night before. This further diminishes their performance on the test. *Id.* Consequently, blacks (and women, to a somewhat lesser degree) are more likely to "disengage" from these tests than whites are. Ronald F. Ferguson, "Teachers' Perceptions and Expectations and the Black-White Test Score Gap," in *The Black-White Test Score Gap*, p. 291. Blacks (and women) are more likely than whites are to decide that their performance on these tests is not important to their personal goals or self-perceptions. *Id.* at 290.

should have the same incentive to do well on employment tests as whites do. Consequently, it is okay for employers to hold black job applicants to the same standards as white job applicants when it comes to *employment* testing, so long as the tests are fair and not racially biased.

One could argue, of course, that the SAT is an "employment test" because it determines whether someone goes to college and thus whether someone eventually gets a good job. But that is not quite true. The SAT determines *which* college someone attends more than it does *whether* someone attends college. Even students with low SAT scores usually get admitted to some college. A significant number of students who score above average on the SAT are no smarter than the ones who score below average, but they are more *status-conscious* and want to go to a *prestigious* college more than the below-average scorers do. So they try harder when preparing for and taking the SAT than the below-average scorers do.

Hopefully these suggestions will help eliminate whatever tendency you might have to "accentuate the negative." Not everyone has this tendency, but some people do.

Exceptions

For most employers, there are only two exceptions to the advice "Be color-blind." One is when you have two job applicants, one white and one black, who are *equally* qualified. If your company is overwhelmingly white, you should probably (although it might depend on circumstances) opt for diversity and hire the black applicant. In addition to the other benefits of diversity (it's good for business), diversity will help you if you or your company are ever sued for race discrimination by a black employee. An overwhelmingly white workforce—or an overwhelmingly white upper echelon within a company—will look suspicious to the EEOC, a judge, or a jury, particularly if you are located in an urban area with a sizeable black population. Although your workforce is not *required* to reflect the demographic percentages that exist in your community, a diverse workforce does tend to show that you do not discriminate against people of color.

But if the two applicants are *not* equally qualified, you should hire the *better*-qualified applicant—the applicant who, based on your objective appraisal of everything you know about him or her, you think would do the job better—whatever color that applicant happens to be. This definition of "better qualified" is, however, flexible. It gives you some leeway. If you have a predominantly white workforce and you have two job applicants, one white and one black, and it is a *very close call* which of them is better qualified, you probably can and should choose the black applicant. This is appropriate *affirmative action*.

What is *in*appropriate affirmative action (and illegal discrimination) is hiring a black person over a white person even though the white person is, by any objective standard, better qualified. There are an increasing number of reverse-discrimination cases: whites suing employers and educational institutions for hiring or admitting blacks who were less qualified than these white applicants. Many whites are winning these cases. The U.S. Supreme Court in *Ricci v. DeStephano* ruled in favor of white firefighters in New Haven who sought to be promoted and who outscored black firefighters on a promotion exam but who, due to the city's desire to promote more black firefighters to supervisory positions and achieve greater diversity, were not promoted.

The second exception comes into play if you have terminated a black employee. You then should consider hiring a black person to replace him or her. It is difficult (not impossible, but difficult) for a terminated black employee to claim that the employer is prejudiced against blacks if the employer replaced that employee with a black person.

Another exception is if an employer is operating under a consent decree or government contract that requires the employer to hire more people of color.

Another exception, of sorts, applies if the government *asks* you to count and report how many women and people of color you employ, as the government asks employers who are required by law to have affirmative action plans (for example, employers with substantial government contracts). You can comply with the government's request. This is not really "considering" race or gender. It is just counting and reporting.

Affirmative Action (is Not the Same as "Reverse Discrimination")

The mere fact that an employer has chosen, or is required, to be an "affirmative action" employer does not mean that the employer must hire less-qualified people of color over better-qualified white employees. *Affirmative action* is a highly misunderstood term. Some think it means "reverse discrimination": hiring a less-qualified job applicant over a more-qualified applicant just because the less-qualified applicant belongs to an historically oppressed or underrepresented group, such as an ethnic minority or the female gender. Many whites and males are adamantly opposed to reverse discrimination.

But the true meaning of affirmative action is simply taking extra steps to ensure that women and minority-group members know about your job openings and feel welcome to apply for and perform jobs in your workplace. Affirmative action of this latter type is perfectly legal, proper, and advisable. Keep in mind that the workforce is not becoming whiter, younger, or more male. It is becoming more female, racially diverse, and older. Diversity is good. The more your workplace reflects these new demographics, the harder it will be for people to accuse you of racism.

Another advantage of diversity is that you can probably attract more customers if you hire a diverse workforce. You might, for example, attract more black customers if you hire more black employees. You might attract more female and Asian customers if you hire more women and Asians. But if you base hiring and promotion decisions on customers' racial preference, or on what you *perceive* to be customers' racial preference, you might run into legal trouble. Consider what happened to national drug-store chain Walgreens in 2007. Walgreens has stores in many poor, inner-city neighborhoods. Walgreens is perhaps the last company you would expect to be sued for race discrimination. But that is exactly what happened. Walgreens was sued by some of its black managers (and by the U.S. Equal Employment Opportunity Commission) for race discrimination in March 2007 because, the suit alleged, Walgreens tried to make sure that its stores in black neighborhoods had black managers.[9] Walgreens was doing what many diversity trainers encourage employers to do. But some black managers sued, alleging that the stores in black neighborhoods generated less revenue, and therefore lower pay for managers, than some stores in white neighborhoods, and they argued that Walgreens should have assigned them to these higher-revenue stores in white neighborhoods. In March 2008, Walgreens settled the suit by agreeing to pay $24 million to a group of some 10,000 black Walgreens employees and former employees.[10]

---

9 http://www.eeoc.gov/press/3-7-07.html.

10 http://www.eeoc.gov/press/3-25-08.html.

The lesson to be learned from the Walgreens case: The best way to avoid being accused of race discrimination is to be color-blind when making employment decisions. The more you notice, think about, and make managerial decisions based on the race or color of your employees, the more legal trouble you potentially bring upon yourself.

For employees who work for the federal government, President Obama's diversity initiative (Executive Order 13583, entitled "Government-Wide Diversity and Inclusion Strategic Plan 2011") says the government should try to achieve diversity—that is, try to build a work force from all segments of society—"while avoiding discrimination for or against any employee or applicant on the basis of race, color, religion, sex (including pregnancy or gender identity), national origin, age, disability, sexual orientation or any other prohibited basis." The best way for private-sector employers to prevent employment discrimination lawsuits is to do the same: Try to achieve diversity while avoiding discrimination for or against an employee or applicant on a prohibited basis. Logic dictates that the best way to do that is to be color-blind; you should be color-blind unless there is a very good, legally valid reason not to be color-blind.

Probably the best way for an employer to achieve diversity is to use "close calls" as an opportunity to become more diverse. A "close call" is when you have two job applicants who are equally qualified. You genuinely do not know which of them would perform the job better. In that circumstance, you have an opportunity to hire the more diverse candidate because all else is equal. However, you should talk to your lawyer about doing this. The law rarely, if ever, says it is OK to discriminate against a job applicant on the basis of skin color—even for the noble purpose of achieving diversity. So employers need to be careful. In any event, these "close calls" have enabled many employers to achieve diversity without getting sued for discrimination.

In general, though, you should, as much as legally possible, treat everyone as though they are members of the same race: the human race.

Diversity Training?

This book neither encourages nor discourages "diversity training."[11] There are many types of diversity training. Some are helpful. Others are counterproductive. If you bring in a diversity trainer, do not express negative, prejudicial, or stereotypical feelings about any group—even if you have such feelings—during training or at any other time. The less you say about race in the workplace, the better. Let the diversity trainer do most if not all the talking. Any such talk on your part can be used against you in court to prove that you are "racist" or "prejudiced." Diversity training is more desirable if done for the purpose of preparing employees to do business in *foreign countries*.

   Be careful if you use the words "culture" and "multiculturalism." People who use those words are usually talking about race and color but think "culture" and "multiculturalism" are more "politically correct" than "race" and "color." Increasingly, the word "culture" is being used to sugar-coat old stereotypes and overgeneralizations. It nearly always means something *other than* culture. If not race or color, then language, national origin, gender, geography, religion, economic class, sexual orientation, or something else. On July 30, 2012, in Israel, U.S. Presidential candidate Mitt Romney explained why, in his opinion, Israel has a more successful economy than the Palestinian Authority has. "Culture makes all the difference," Romney said. "And as I come here and I look out over this city and consider the accomplishments of the people of this nation, I recognize the power of at least culture and a few other things." He added, "As you come here and you see the GDP per capita, for instance, in Israel, which is about $21,000, and compare that with the GDP per capita just across the areas managed by the Palestinian Authority, which is more like $10,000 per capita, you notice such a dramatically stark difference in economic vitality. And that is also between other countries that are near or next to each other. Chile and Ecuador, Mexico and the United States."[12]

---

11   For an interesting perspective on this topic, see Lisa Takeuchi Cullen, "Diversity Training Doesn't Work," *Time*, Apr. 26, 2007 (a study conducted by some sociologists from Harvard, the University of California at Berkeley, and the University of Minnesota concluded that "diversity training has little or no effect on the racial and gender mix of a company's top ranks").

12   "Romney Trip Raises Sparks at a 2nd Stop," *New York Times*, July 30, 2012, retrieved from http://www.nytimes.com/2012/07/31/us/politics/romney-angers-palestinians-with-comments-in-israel.html?pagewanted=all (last visited Mar. 14, 2013).

Whatever Romney meant by "culture," it sounded to Palestinians as though Romney is saying some races and ethnicities are smarter or harder-working than others. The remarks drew a swift rebuke from Palestinian leaders. Saeb Erekat, a senior aide to President Mahmoud Abbas of the Palestinian Authority, called Romney's remarks racist. "It is a racist statement and this man doesn't realize that the Palestinian economy cannot reach its potential because there is an Israeli occupation," Erekat said. Romney responded that he (Romney) was not speaking about Palestinian culture but rather was saying that the choices a society makes have a profound impact on the economy and vitality of that society. This is a good example of why you should be careful when using the word "culture": It can have different meanings to different people.

"Culture" and "multiculturalism" are used to justify comments like, "Germans are very punctual but Italians tend to be late; it's their culture." "That is part of the male culture." "People in New York eat dinner late; that is their culture." "Asians do not like to make eye contact; it is against their culture." Korean culture is this or that. Puerto Ricans like this or that. Irish, Jews, Southerners, Northerners, whatever.

Ignore such generalizations. People are people. Some Germans are punctual and some are late. Some New Yorkers eat dinner late, others eat early. To the extent that people think or communicate differently from one another, it has nothing to do with their race, color, ethnicity, gender, age, religion, genetics, or ability/disability. Someone can be your exact age, ethnicity, profession, gender, religion, economic background, and live on your street, but you will not necessarily like him or her or agree with him or her on anything. Conversely, someone different from you racially, religiously, professionally, economically, and in every other "cultural" way might be a close friend of yours and agree with you on most things. In the workplace, the less you think about and talk about race, color, ethnicity, gender, age, religion, genetics, and disability, the better. Keep in mind the words of Marcel Marceau, who as a pantomime artist performed silently onstage but spoke normally offstage. He said, "There is no French way of laughing and no American way of crying."[13]

---

13 Obituary, "Marcel Marceau, Renowned Mime, Dies at 84," *New York Times*, Sept. 24, 2007.

Don't Talk About Race and Skin Color Except When Necessary

When people—even people who are strong supporters of civil rights and racial equality—comment about a race or ethnicity other than their own, their comment is likely to lead to hard feelings and negative consequences *unless the comment is 100 percent positive.* Consider the comment of 1984 Democratic vice-presidential nominee Geraldine Ferraro, who was white and from New York, during the 2008 presidential primaries. Ferraro had a long, distinguished record of supporting civil rights and racial equality. While supporting her then-New York senator, Hillary Clinton, in the 2008 presidential primaries, Ferraro, in a casual conversation with a reporter from a small newspaper, commented that Clinton's main opponent for the Democratic presidential nomination, Barack Obama, benefited in the presidential campaign as a result of being black. Ferraro said Obama did not have as much experience as Clinton and said that if a white candidate had the same amount of experience as Obama then had (in early 2008), the white candidate would not have received as many votes for the Democratic presidential nomination as Obama was receiving. Likewise, Ferraro admitted, *she* (Ferraro) benefited in 1984 from being a *woman.* A *man* with her level of experience in 1984 would *not* have been nominated for vice-president, she said. Obama, argued Ferraro, was receiving enormous numbers of votes from the black community and also from white voters who believe that white people should atone for the sins of slavery and discrimination by electing a black President, just as Ferraro received large numbers of votes from women in 1984. Ferraro's comment was not a *negative* comment about blacks, but it was not a *100% positive* comment about blacks, either. Because it was not a 100% positive comment about blacks, Ferraro was harshly criticized by blacks and some whites.

Obama responded that being black is *not* an advantage when running for national office but rather is a *dis*advantage.

Who was correct, Ferraro or Obama? Was being black an *advantage* for Obama or a *dis*advantage?[14] I will not even try to answer that question. Many

---

14 A similar question was asked in 2008 about Republican vice presidential nominee Sarah Palin: Did being a woman help her or hurt her in her political career? On one hand, it can be argued that being female helped her because a male with the same résumé as hers—four years as mayor of a city of only 5,000 people and two years as governor of a state (Alaska) that has fewer people than almost any other state—would not have been considered for Vice President. On the other hand, Palin's wardrobe and parenting ability ("Will she be able to be a good mother to her infant child while serving as Vice

blacks would answer the question one way, many whites would answer it the other way. If this were 1963 rather than 2013, all blacks and nearly all whites would agree that being black is a disadvantage when running for President of the United States. 1963 was before most of the civil rights laws were passed. In 1964 civil rights laws were passed that give blacks equal rights in employment, voting, housing, and public accommodations, and that require many employers to take affirmative steps ("affirmative action") to ensure that blacks and whites have equal employment opportunity. Whether those laws have worked is debatable. Many whites today (2013) believe that those laws have worked and believe that affirmative action has given blacks an advantage over whites. Many blacks disagree with that. There is no consensus about who is correct and who is incorrect in this debate. This debate should be avoided as much as possible in the workplace.

Can racial and ethnic diversity be achieved without *talking about* race and ethnicity? I will answer that question this way: Employers should make a strong effort to achieve racial diversity *except* when such effort leads to race *discrimination* (*race discrimination* being defined as treating an employee—white, black, or other—less favorably due to his or her race or ethnicity). The more that race, ethnicity, gender, age, religion, genetics, disability, and sexual orientation are discussed in the workplace, the more lawsuits there are. As a University of Maryland historian has observed, when people speak about race,

> It's not an easy subject for black people or white people. . . . It is extremely easy for people to misspeak. People . . . sometimes use the wrong words or are condescending or seem to be condescending when they're trying to be honest. It's easy for people to take offense when the wrong language is used, particularly when they've got within them a lot of anger. . . . In those circumstances, it's often better to say nothing.[15]

President?") were questioned by many people who would not have asked such questions about a man. A similar question was asked in 2009 about U.S. Supreme Court nominee Sonia Sotomayor: Did being Latino help her or hurt her in her career?

15   Comment of Ira Berlin, professor of African-American history at the University of Maryland, quoted in Janny Scott, "What Politicians Say When They Talk About Race," *New York Times*, Mar. 23, 2008.

In 2009 U.S. attorney general Eric Holder stated that America is a nation of "cowards" when it comes to talking about race. He says Americans are afraid to talk about race. He is largely correct. Many Americans are afraid to talk about race. But they are afraid for good reason: If they talk about race and someone gets offended by the talk, someone might sue and collect a large sum of money in the lawsuit.

The bottom line is that employers should be color-blind except if and when they have very good, legally valid reason not to be color-blind.

The civil rights laws essentially require employers to be race-blind, color-blind, ethnicity-blind, genetics-blind, and, to a very large extent, gender-blind, age-blind, and religion-blind. If people don't want race-blindness, color-blindness, ethnicity-blindness, gender-blindness, age-blindness, genetics-blindness, and religion-blindness in the workplace, they should lobby to change the civil rights laws. But until the civil rights laws are changed, the civil rights laws, as they are currently written, should be obeyed. You can try to *change* the law through the political process if you think the law is wrong, but *until* the law is changed, you should *obey* it. The civil rights laws as they are currently written essentially (that is, with very few exceptions) require race-blindness, color-blindness, ethnicity-blindness, gender-blindness, age-blindness[16], genetics-blindness, and religion-blindness in employment.

Over the past 50 years or so, there have been countless conversations, dialogues, workshops, and other well-intentioned discussions about race, but it is unclear whether they have helped end race discrimination in the workplace. The best way to end race discrimination in the workplace is to *be color-blind*. Efforts to be color-blind will not always succeed, but conversations, dialogues, and workshops on race never, or hardly ever, succeed. In the workplace, being color-blind, or at least trying to be color-blind, is more apt to succeed than talking about race is.

---

16   In most states, a person must be at least 40 years old to sue for age discrimination. In a few states, anyone can sue for age discrimination, so long as he or she is old enough to be legally hired for the job.

Summary

This discussion ("Be color-blind") boils down to the following simple advice:

- When firing, laying off, demoting, or disciplining employees, or when setting pay or other terms and conditions of employment, be totally color-blind. In other words, when taking *negative* or *neutral* action, be color-blind.
- When recruiting, hiring, or promoting employees, be color-blind except when the qualifications of a black candidate and a white candidate are *equal* or *very close* (too close to call), in which case you probably (there might be an occasional exception to this; talk to your lawyer about particular situations) should opt for diversity: If you have a shortage of black employees at that particular job level, hire the black candidate. In other words, when taking *positive* action, you ordinarily (again, there might be an occasional exception to this; talk to your lawyer about particular situations) can, when the qualifications of two job applicants are equal or very close (too close to call), give some consideration to color. But even so, try not to *talk about* race or color.
- Do not talk about race or racial differences except when necessary.

Chapter Two

Prevent Gender Discrimination

Treat Men and Women the Same
(With a Few Very Minor Exceptions)

Try not to differentiate in any way between men and women in the workplace. Besides referring to a male as "he" or "Mr." and a female as "she" or "Ms." (or, if she prefers, "Miss" or "Mrs."), and besides providing separate restrooms for men and women and allowing men and women to dress differently, try to pretend that all your workers are the same gender: the "worker" gender. The law says you should treat women and men the same in the workplace unless the woman is pregnant and close to giving birth or has just given birth, in which case she has some rights that men don't have (see "Pregnancy, Adoption, and Maternity Leave," pages 37-40 below), or if there is a job that can only be performed by one gender. For example, if you need someone to model women's clothes, you can restrict your hiring to women for that position. That is called a "bona fide occupational qualification," or "BFOQ." Use gender-neutral language in oral and written communication. Don't call women over the age of 18 "girls."

The announcement in January 2013 by U.S. Secretary of Defense Leon Panetta that women will now be permitted to serve in combat will, I think, do more to achieve equality for women (equality with men) in the *workplace,* not just the battlefield, than any other event in U.S. history. With very, very few exceptions, there is no reason to treat women differently than men.

This advice to treat men and women the same might upset some people. After years of trying—successfully—to prove that men and women have *equal* abilities (except perhaps that the average man has a little more upper-body strength than the average woman has), some people (some women and some men) are now saying that women *think, communicate,* and *manage employees* differently than men do.

Employers should ignore such talk. For thousands of years, one major cause of discrimination against women was the belief that women think differently than men. That belief resulted in women earning less than men and being subordinate to men in many types of employment. In the 1970s and '80s, women rejected that belief. As a result, women made great strides toward achieving full equality with men in the workplace. Today, however, that belief is back in vogue in some circles.

Keep in mind that that belief—the belief that women think, communicate, and manage employees differently than men do—is held and expressed mainly by *authors, lecturers,* and *college professors,* not managers. *Managers* should not hold or express that belief. Managers who express that belief or base their managerial decisions on that belief risk being sued for sex discrimination.

If you are a manager, you should *ignore* all statements and literature that argue that women think, communicate, or manage differently than men do. Such arguments are generalizations that ignore the fact that not all men are the same and not all women are the same. Moreover, these generalizations are usually based on immeasurable characteristics and anecdotal observations. These generalizations are nothing new. They are as old as time. They have historically *hurt* women more than *helped* women in the quest for equality. Examples of such generalizations are: "Women use their instincts and emotional intelligence more than men do. Men just use logic." "Women prefer working in groups; men prefer working alone." "Women are less assertive than men." "Women are more nurturing than men." "Women are better communicators than men are." "Men are better negotiators than women are." "Men don't ask directions." "Men don't cry." "Men's brains are 'hard-wired,' which makes them less comfortable expressing their emotions." "Men can only think about one thing at a time; women can think about many things at a time." "Women think 'outside the box' better than men do."

The people who make such statements mean well. They are trying to empower women. But in fact they are doing the opposite: they are perpetuating old stereotypes about women, such as the stereotype that men use logic more than instinct while women use instinct more than logic. Remember the old stereotype of a woman complaining to her husband, "I hate it when you're logical"? These people are claiming that that is true: men are too logical. "Men should use less logic and more feelings and intuition, like women do," these people say. Such statements lead to legal trouble. If a *male manager* were to say "Men think logically more than women do," he would be accused of "degrading" and "devaluing" women. He might get sued for sex discrimination. He would face an uphill battle in court.

You should *treat men and women the same* and *not talk about gender differences at all*. In fact, you should assume (except perhaps in some very rare circumstances) that in terms of *job performance*, there are no gender differences.

Women managers who talk about how women are better at one thing or another than men are (such as having better "intuition," "listening skills," or "communication skills" than men have) risk being sued for sex discrimination by male subordinates and rejected male job applicants. They might even be sued for creating a "hostile work environment" toward men. Women should avoid such talk. Such talk will cause men to file sex discrimination lawsuits.

Men and Women Are Both from Earth[17]

Managers should reject all generalizations that men are this and women are that. Such generalizations are no different than generalizations claiming that white people are this and black people are that. Such generalizations only lead to trouble. Such generalizations come dangerously close to saying, "Women are better than men" or "Men are smarter than women." That is no different from saying, "Blacks are better than whites" or "Whites are smarter than blacks" or some other rash, racist, sexist generalization. It is dangerous stuff. As Carol Gilligan warned in her famous book on male-female psychological differences, *In a Different Voice: Psychological Theory and*

---

17   "Men and Women Are Both from Earth" was a headline in the *New York Times Book Review*, April 11, 1999, p. 19.

Women's Development, "it is difficult to say 'different' without saying 'better' or 'worse.'"[18]

You should not assume anything about a person's thinking just because of his or her gender, race, color, national origin, age, disability, religion, or sexual orientation. Many blacks are smarter than many whites, many whites are smarter than many blacks, many men are smarter than many women, and many women are smarter than many men. That is all we know. That does not tell us anything about a *particular* black person, white person, male, or female. Don't lump people together just because they are the same gender, race, color, national origin, age, ability/disability, religion, or sexual orientation. Regard each person as an *individual* who may be very different from other people of his or her gender, race, color, national origin, age, ability/disability, religion, or sexual orientation.

Be skeptical of the "studies" these people mention. There are all kinds of "studies" showing that women are different than men, blacks are different than whites, old people are different than young people, etc. Hitler relied on such "studies." All racist, sexist thinkers rely on such studies. That is because such "studies"—especially the ones based on IQ tests and combined SAT scores— tend to make white males look smarter than women (in math and science, anyway) and blacks. For every "study" showing that women have some advantage over men, there is a study, or test scores, showing that men have some advantage over women. "In One Ear, Without the Other" was an article that appeared some years ago.[19] It was about an Indiana University School of Medicine study that showed that men listen with the left side of their brains while women listen with both sides of their brains. The first line of the article read, "Score one for exasperated women: New research suggests men really do listen with just half their brains." Numerous women, and some men, went on talk shows and declared that this study proves once and for all that men "just don't listen." But men countered by saying that in reality the study shows that men *have more brainpower* than women: Men need only *half* their brains to hear as much as women hear with their *whole* brains. Managers should ignore such studies and debates.

---

18   Cambridge: Harvard University Press, 1993 ed., p. 14.

19   *Springfield* [Mass.] *Union-News,* Nov, 29, 2000, p. A1. The study was widely reported around the nation, but different media outlets used different headlines. On *webmd.com,* the headline reads, "Men Listen, But With Only Half a Brain," http://www.webmd.com/news/20001128/men-listen-with-only-half-brain (last visited Mar. 14, 2013).

Here is another example. An article in the December 2007 *Harvard Business Review* discussed a study that concluded that women are more apt to accept the first salary offer from an employer than to negotiate with the employer for a higher salary. The article said, "[W]omen and men negotiate differently for pay raises, promotions, and salaries. The key difference: Many women don't negotiate at all."[20] A manager—male or female—might read that article and decide not to put women on any negotiating team. According to the study, or to the article about the study, women are too willing to accept what is offered rather than negotiate for more. A manager (male or female) might read that article and decide to offer lower salaries to women than to men, believing, as the article asserts, that women are more likely to accept a lower salary than men are. Such managerial thinking is discriminatory and can lead to discrimination lawsuits.

With all due respect to the people who conduct and write about such studies and debates, *employers* should *disregard* such studies and debates. Such studies and debates lead to feuds and discrimination. They create friction rather than unity. There is often a fine line between *statistics* and *stereotypes*. There are studies and statistics showing that certain ethnic groups have more athletic ability, mathematical ability, and some other abilities and traits than other ethnic groups do. "Study finds ethnic link to math test scores," was a headline a few years ago.[21] "How race affects smoking," which cites a study showing that certain ethnic groups have more difficulty quitting smoking than other ethnic groups do, is another.[22] Whether there is or is not a link between ethnicity and math scores, or between race and quitting smoking, and whether that link, if it exists, is due to one factor or another factor, employers should ignore it. Employers who rely on such studies and let these studies guide their behavior at work are asking for trouble—*legal* trouble. *Big* legal trouble. Employers should disregard all studies, books, seminars, and discussions that show intellectual or emotional differences between men and women, whites and blacks, old people and young people, etc.

---

20   Elizabeth Agnvall, "Women and Negotiation: Research Indicates That Basic Reluctance to Ask Contributes to Women Lagging Men in Pay," *Harvard Business Review*, Dec. 2007, at 69 (discussing research conducted by Carnegie Mellon University economics professor Linda Babcock).

21   *Springfield* [Mass.] *Union-News*, Apr. 11, 2001, p. B1.

22   *Time*, Mar. 10, 2008, at 48; retrieved from http://www.time.com/time/magazine/article/0,9171,1718560,00.html (last visited Mar. 14, 2013).

Moreover, many of these studies, books, seminars, and discussions are *contradicted* by other studies, books, seminars, and discussions. A common generalization, for example, is that women are more talkative than men. But a study conducted between 1998 and 2004 and reported in *Science* magazine in 2007 shows that women are *not* more talkative than men. "Women and men both use on average about 16,000 words per day, with very large individual differences around this mean."[23]

Employers should disregard statements to the effect that men were "brought up" one way and women the other way. Some men were, some weren't. Some women were, some weren't. Furthermore, not every man and woman does what they were "brought up" to do. A common generalization about men, for example, is that they don't cry. They were "brought up" to stifle their emotions rather than cry. But is this generalization true? Consider this April 19, 2001, *Boston Globe* headline: "Cowboys Shed Tears as Stock Yard Ends Era." When the Union Stock Yards in San Antonio, Texas, closed after 112 years in business, "Hardscrabble Texas cowboys wept as the final gavel fell," according to the article.

So much for generalizations. Not only do *ordinary* men cry, *ultimate* men— *cowboys*—cry. Current U.S. House speaker John Boehner has openly cried with emotion in several TV appearances. So have many male athletes.

In short, employers should *disregard all generalizations about men and all generalizations about women*. Generalizing is stereotyping, and stereotyping leads to discrimination. The more you discriminate or differentiate between men and women or between one race and another race, the more legal trouble you potentially bring upon yourself. You should not differentiate between men and women except you can differentiate in the four aspects listed above—dress codes,[24] restrooms, maternity leave, and bona fide occupational qualification ("BFOQ")—or between whites and people of color. To "differentiate" is basically to *discriminate*, and *discrimination* is usually *against* a group, or *in favor of*

---

23   Matthias R. Mehl et als (2007), "Are Women Really More Talkative Than Men?" *Science*, July 6, 2007, at 82.

24   In Connecticut, Massachusetts, and a few other states, a male employee might have the legal right to dress like a woman, and a female employee might have the legal right to dress like a man, at work. I'll explain this in the section about sexual orientation discrimination. Advocates for the LGBT (lesbians, gays, bisexuals, and transgendered) community have persuaded lawmakers in some states to enact legislation prohibiting employers from requiring male employees to dress like men. Few employers object to a woman wearing pants, but many employers object to a man wearing a skirt or dress, especially at work. See the discussion on pages 66-67.

one group *at the expense of* another group. The "BFOQ" exception to the rule that men and women must be treated the same is a very narrow exception. Only if *all* of the members of a gender (*all* men or *all* women) are unqualified for a job can you restrict your hiring to the other gender.

If college professors wish to conduct experiments to see if men think differently than women, that is okay. If teachers and trainers want to help people learn to value or even just tolerate diversity, that too is okay. Everyone should value or at least tolerate diversity. In your *behavior*, however—at least in the workplace—*you should treat men and women the same.*

For all these reasons, this book recommends against diversity training that deals with gender (or religion or sexual orientation, for that matter). Perhaps if you have some employees who do business in certain *foreign countries* where, by law, women are treated differently than men, those employees might benefit from such training as it relates to those specific countries.

As for brawn, few jobs require such enormous physical strength that women cannot perform them as well as men. The only jobs I can think of, offhand, in which women have difficulty competing with men are professional sports. There are no women playing in the National Football League, Major League Baseball, the National Basketball Association, or the National Hockey League; and no women boxing against men, playing tennis against men, or playing golf against men, in serious professional matches (except in mixed pairs). A few years ago, two women (Annika Sorenstam and Michelle Wie) competed against men in professional golf, with little success. These leagues do not *exclude* women. Women can try out for these teams if they want, and if they beat out enough of the men, they will make the team. But that has not happened yet. In any event, major-league sports comprise only a tiny fraction of jobs. There are plenty of other physical-labor jobs, and women can perform almost all of them as well as men can. Keep in mind the enormous physical ability displayed by women soldiers in Iraq and Afghanistan over the past few years.

If you need to fill a physical labor job, do not assume, just because an applicant is female, that she is weaker than the male applicants. You can, if you want, conduct strength and endurance tests if such tests are job-related. Everyone, male and female, will take the tests. The strongest applicants will get the jobs, be they male or female.

Of course, you are not *required* to conduct such tests. But if a 150-pound man and a 150-pound woman apply for a job, don't assume that the man is stronger. Let them both test for the job. The test does not have to be elaborate or lengthy. It can be short and simple. Don't have a height, weight, or strength requirement unless you have substantial proof that a certain height, weight, or strength is necessary to perform the job. Some police and fire departments might still have height or weight requirements, but that is government (public-sector) employment. Sometimes the rules are a bit different in public-sector employment than in private-sector employment.

If a test procedure screens out a protected group (for example, if all or almost all women, or all or almost all blacks, flunk the test, and all or almost all men, or all or almost all whites, pass the test), you should explore whether there is an equally effective alternative selection procedure that has less adverse impact on women or blacks, and if so, adopt the alternative procedure. You should explore whether another test would predict job performance but not disproportionately exclude women or blacks. To ensure that a test or selection procedure remains predictive of success in a job, you should keep abreast of changes in job requirements and should update the test specifications or selection procedures accordingly. You should ensure that tests and selection procedures are not adopted casually by managers who know little about these processes. A test or selection procedure can be an effective management tool, but no test or selection procedure should be implemented without an understanding of its effectiveness and limitations for the organization, its appropriateness for a specific job, and whether it can be appropriately administered and scored.[25]

The law generally (there might be an occasional exception to this) allows you to discriminate on the basis of physical attractiveness. You can hire a pretty woman over a not-so-pretty woman if you want, and you can hire a handsome man over a not-so-handsome man if you want. However, if you do, you must make sure that you do not consciously or subconsciously discriminate on the basis of gender, race, ethnicity, age, or religion. If you are more apt to judge *women* as good looking than you are *men*, and thus you are more apt to hire women than men for a particular type of job, that is gender discrimination and is illegal. If you are more apt to judge white people as good looking than you are black people, or more apt to judge young people as good looking than you are old people, that is race discrimination or age

---

25   U.S. Equal Employment Opportunity Commission, *Employment Test and Selection Procedures*, http://www.eeoc.gov/policy/docs/factemployment_procedures.html (last visited Mar. 14, 2013).

discrimination and is illegal. Keep up with developments in the law on this topic. There are efforts being made in some states to enact legislation that would altogether prohibit discrimination based on physical appearance. Thus, it is possible that sometime soon employers in one or more states will be prohibited from discriminating on the basis of an employee's physical attractiveness.

No law requires that your workforce reflect the gender ratio (roughly 50-50) of the general population. As a matter of common sense, however, an all-male or nearly all-male workforce does raise the suspicion that you discriminate against women. If you have such a workforce and a male and a female with roughly equal qualifications apply for a job, you should probably hire the female. The more women you employ, especially in high places, the harder it is to accuse you of discriminating against women.

And be on the lookout for *men* claiming they are being discriminated against by women in overwhelmingly female workplaces. If a man with good secretarial skills applies for a secretarial job at your company and all ten of your secretaries are female, and you reject the man for the job, don't be surprised if he sues for sex discrimination. He might even win.

Pregnancy, Adoption, and Maternity Leave

The law generally regards pregnancy discrimination as a form of sex discrimination. However, most states have their own employment laws pertaining to pregnancy, adoption, and maternity leave, so it is difficult to generalize about them in a short book such as this. You should look at the laws of your particular state.

Under federal law, employers with 15 or more employees are required to treat pregnancy the same way they would treat any short-term illness.[26] Many states' laws go further: They require employers to allow pregnant women time off to give birth and recuperate (this is called "maternity leave") even if they would not ordinarily allow a male employee or a not-pregnant female employee that much time off for illness. (Unless the law or an employer's particular arrangement with his or her employees provides otherwise, the employer does not have to pay the woman during this period.) And if the employer has 50 or more employees, an employee who is the parent (male or

---

26   42 U.S.C. § 2000e(k).

female) of a newborn or soon-to-be-born child might be entitled to up to 12 weeks off, under the federal Family and Medical Leave Act (FMLA), and possibly more than 12 weeks under the family and medical leave acts of some states (such as Connecticut). Pregnancy-related illnesses (such as morning sickness) ordinarily do not qualify as "disabilities" under the Americans with Disabilities Act, so the ADA provides little protection to pregnant women. Some pregnancy-related illnesses may qualify as "serious health conditions" entitling a pregnant woman (and possibly her husband or boyfriend) to FMLA leave, but others will not.

Employers should not discriminate against pregnant women or women who might become pregnant. Not only is it illegal, it is counterproductive. Although pregnancy might occasionally divert a woman's time and attention away from her work, and giving birth will keep her out of the workplace for a few months, pregnancy and childbirth also give her an added incentive to do a good job for you. She now has another mouth to feed. She will need more money than a childless person does. She will be motivated to work harder to earn that extra money. She might seek a promotion or pay raise. The same is true of *men* whose *wives* get pregnant. These men have more incentive, too.

Thus, discrimination against women due to their pregnancy or potential pregnancy is bad not only from a legal standpoint but also from a business standpoint. Many working mothers have very good child-care arrangements. According to *Journal of the American Board of Family Medicine*, 58 percent of employed, first-time mothers giving birth in the United States between 2001 and 2003 returned to work within three months after giving birth,[27] and according to a 1999 edition of *Working Mother* magazine (I don't know if the percentage has changed since 1999), 83 percent of employed, first-time mothers returned to work within six months after giving birth.[28] Many companies are allowing women (and men) to bring their babies to work and are providing onsite child care facilities.[29] Many women want to earn as much money as their husbands earn. Equal earnings mean equal power

---

27   C. Randall Clinch, et als (2009), "Characteristics of Mother-Provider Interactions Surrounding Postpartum Return to Work," *Journal of the American Board of Family Medicine* 22(5), 498-506.

28   June 1999, p. 32.

29   See "Who's the Boss? Offices That Let Parents Bring Their Babies to Work Generate Some Surprising Reactions," *Time*, Jan. 14, 2008, at 61.

in the marital relationship. More and more men are content with having *less* power than their wives have. If their wives have successful careers, these men are willing to spend more time at home with the children. If the woman has a high-paying job, she and her husband might decide that *her* career will come first. Many male executives say, "I wish my wife had a high-paying job; then I could stay home more. I'd rather be home with my kids than working so hard." As Jane Bryant Quinn said in a column about married couples, "When she brings home more bacon, he makes more beds."[30]

What can pregnant women do to reduce the likelihood they will be discriminated against? Here is some good advice given to pregnant job seekers by Elaine Varelas, a career counselor in Boston, in the "Job Doc" section of the *Boston Globe*:

> Mother Nature lets you keep the news private for some time, and during those months I would network and interview without disclosing your situation. Some employers might not agree with this advice. I can tell you that the disclosure of this news—legal or not—does affect how people view you as a candidate. As a good job seeker, you need to spend time with a potential employer so they can see what you have to offer and how you would fit into their culture before they are faced with any obstacles - which a maternity represents to some employers.
>
> As you move into second and third interviews, and the second and third trimesters, you are right to feel the need to begin disclosing your situation, and a very strong statement about your plans to return to work. If this is not your first child, hiring managers need to know that you returned to work after your previous leaves. Potential employers need to hear about the plans you have for child care and backup care. They need to hear that you have sisters or close friends who have also gone back to work after having children and that you learned a great deal about how you will handle the situation from them.
>
> Some employers will assume you have no idea how

---

30   Jane Bryant Quinn, "Which Spouse Has More Paycheck Power?" *Springfield* [Mass.] *Sunday Republican*, May 30, 1999, p. F3.

you will feel leaving your newborn, and they will be very hesitant about investing training dollars in what they view as a high-risk hire. Depending on how far along you are, you may be able to negotiate a project or temporary arrangement with them prior to having your child, with a formal start date following your leave.

I have seen some great hires of talented women while they were pregnant. The managers and organizations who took this "risk" were able to get exceptional employees with unbelievable loyalty.[31]

I think that is generally good advice, although it is difficult to generalize about what employers think and what job seekers should do. It will depend on your particular circumstances.

One More Tip for Employers

If you fire a woman, consider hiring a woman to replace her, especially if you have a mostly male workforce. It will be much harder for the fired woman to claim sex discrimination. You don't *have to* replace her with a woman, but you should consider it, especially if you have few women employees in that job category.

---

31   Job Doc, *Boston Globe*, May 31, 2009.

Chapter Three

Prevent Sexual Harassment

There are two types of sexual harassment, but it is not always easy to distinguish one from the other. Nor is there much reason to. You can be sued for either. The two types are 1) *quid pro quo* sexual harassment and 2) sexually hostile work environment.

Quid pro quo sexual harassment

Quid pro quo sexual harassment occurs when a boss makes employment decisions based on whether a subordinate will have sexual (or romantic) relations with him. It need not be explicit (such as, "Go to bed with me or you're fired"). If a boss asks a secretary for a date and she turns him down, and a year later he fires her for being late for the fifteenth time (after giving her stern warnings the twelfth, thirteenth, and fourteenth times), don't be surprised if she sues him and the company for *quid pro quo* sexual harassment. She will claim that the *real* reason he fired her is that she refused to go out with him a year earlier. If she does date him for awhile, and the relationship then turns sour, and he fires her for being late the fifteenth time, she will claim that the *real* reason he fired her was that the relationship turned sour.

For that reason, supervisors generally should not date or have sex with their subordinates, or even try to. If you are physically attracted to your secretary or other subordinate, try to get him or her off your mind in that respect. Picture her or him less attractive. Do whatever it takes to avoid thinking of him or her in a sexual way. There is too great a chance that such a romantic relationship, even if occurs for awhile, will eventually end. When it ends, you will never be able to discipline or fire that subordinate without being accused of *sexual harassment* or *"retaliation."* It is illegal to fire an employee in retaliation for their complaining about sexual harassment. There is also the chance of blackmail—an employee showing an interest in you, hoping you will grab the bait so she or he can accuse you of sexual harassment.

If you find yourself becoming attracted to a subordinate, remember the words of former Secretary of State Henry Kissinger when he was asked why a rather average-looking man like himself was able to attract gorgeous women: "Power is the ultimate aphrodisiac." What he meant was, if he were a nobody, gorgeous women would have no interest in him. Only because he held a *position of power* were they interested.

What does this have to do with sexual harassment? Plenty. You have probably heard the cliché, "Sexual harassment isn't about sex, it's about power." Kissinger proved that that cliché is *half* true: Sexual harassment is about power. But it is also about sex. In fact, it is usually more about sex than about power. When a male boss expresses a sexual interest in a female subordinate, the boss is not just showing off his power. (For the purpose of this explanation, I will use the example of a male boss and a female subordinate, but it could just as easily be the other way around.) He is thinking about sex, not power. His power, however, might make certain things happen. It might make him a bit more confident that the subordinate will accept his invitation for a date. It might also make the subordinate more interested in the boss, not because she fears the consequences of turning him down, but because she *genuinely* finds him more attractive than she would if he had no "power."

Women will sometimes flirt with or be interested in a man who is their boss yet would not be interested in him if he were of equal rank to them. They are attracted to his "power" more than they are attracted to him, really. Not that they are looking for anything in return. They are not necessarily looking for a raise or promotion or job security. They are simply intrigued by the thought of dating a man with "power," just as men are intrigued by dating women with power.

This dynamic is indeed gender-neutral. Men are sexually attracted to powerful women just as women are sexually attracted to powerful men.

Power is, as Kissinger said, the ultimate aphrodisiac *regardless of which gender holds the power*. Men are often attracted to women executives and women politicians who would not be so attractive to these men if these women were waitresses and sales clerks. These men are also attracted to waitresses and sales clerks, but a waitress or sales clerk might have to be more physically attractive than a woman executive or politician to arouse sexual interest in these men. Some women probably think that women with power are a turn*off* to men. Maybe *some* men are turned off by them, but many men are attracted to them, just as many women are attracted to men with power.

So if you are a male boss and you think the attraction between you and a female subordinate is mutual, ask yourself this question: If you were not her boss, would she be attracted to you? If your answer is no, do not attempt to romance her. She is intrigued by your power, and is possibly, though not necessarily, trying to get ahead in your company. A male subordinate might try to do the same with a female boss. There is usually no legal problem if that subordinate does get ahead in your company. But if that subordinate does not get ahead in your company, that subordinate will blame *you* and might sue you and your company for sexual harassment. Do not succumb to temptation without thinking through all the ramifications.

If you are quite certain that the subordinate is genuinely interested in you and would be even if you were not his or her boss, then nonetheless tread very carefully. It is legally unwise to date a subordinate, but if you really want to, try to make sure that the attraction is mutual and has nothing to do with the power you have over her. If she has given you no hint whatsoever that she is interested in you, don't ask her out.

If you do ask out a subordinate and she says no, or she gives you some lame excuse ("Uh, I have company coming in this weekend"), don't ask again. Forget about it. If it doesn't happen easily, give up. Don't be persistent in trying to get a date with a subordinate. You are asking for trouble. If she or he turns you down or gives you an excuse, don't pout or walk off in a huff. Any anger or frustration you exhibit will be noticed and can be used against you by that subordinate if you ever have to fire, demote, or take some other type of adverse employment action against her. She will say it is because she turned you down for a date.

What about dating *co*-workers, that is, people of the same rank as you? That is usually okay. Just remember, though, the higher up you are in the company, the fewer the employees you can safely attempt to romance.

Should your company adopt a no-dating rule, that is, a rule that says no employee can date a co-employee? Or a rule requiring the two employees (or just the subordinate employee) to sign a form indicating that the relationship is totally consensual? There is rarely a good reason for such rules, but it might depend on the circumstances.

If an employee complains to you that she is being bothered by or pursued too aggressively by a co-worker and asks you to intercede and tell the pursuer to stop, do so. Whenever you receive a complaint that someone is being sexually harassed, ask the victim *what she wants you to do about it*. If she is unsure, tell her there is little or nothing you can do about it—other than reminding all your employees of your sexual harassment policy—until she decides what she wants you to do about it. Don't be afraid to tell her to first try to work the problem out herself with the harasser. The harasser will usually be angrier if the victim goes *over his head* or *behind his back* (that is, complains to the harasser's boss or to other people in the company) than if the victim complains to the harasser directly. Nearly all men will stop harassing a woman once the woman makes *absolutely clear* to him that she is not interested in him. The problem is when the woman gives *mixed signals* or has already had a lengthy, intimate relationship with the man. Quite often a woman will call a lawyer and complain that a male boss or co-worker has been harassing her for a long time. She usually wants to know if she has a good sexual harassment case.

> "Did you ever accept one of his invitations?" the lawyer will ask.
> "Yeah, a few times," the woman will reply.
> "When was the last time?" the lawyer will ask.
> "Last week," she will reply.
> "If he's so bad, why did you accept?"
> "I didn't know he was that bad. Actually, we went out a number of times. But I don't want to go out with him anymore. I want him to leave me alone. He has a problem with that."
> "Did you feel in any way coerced to go out with him?"
> "Not really."

These cases are like domestic violence cases in which the man pushes the woman around for the twelfth time, she forgives him for the twelfth time, and then the thirteenth time he *really* gets violent. If she had dumped him the first or second time, he'd be long gone and have forgotten about her. But after twelve times, these men become like dogs who keep finding food that a sympathetic person left for them. That person will have great difficulty getting rid of the dog now. The dog is so accustomed to the food that the dog will growl, bite, and bark for the food now. The dog thinks he has a "right" to that person's food. The dog thinks he "owns" that person.

Be patient, however. If the harassment victim needs your assistance to formulate a plan to deal with the problem (such as when she is being harassed by a supervisor), assist her. Many states have laws prescribing what an employer should do when an employee complains of sexual harassment. Check your state's laws for guidance on this.

Should your company adopt a policy strictly prohibiting supervisors and executives from dating subordinates? That is a tough call. Such a policy reduces the risk of sexual harassment lawsuits but might not be good human resource management. The opportunity for romance is an important— though unofficial—employee "benefit." A company where unmarried men and women have opportunities to find romance will attract more and better job applicants and have better employee morale than a company that prohibits such opportunities.

I emphasize the word *unmarried*, however. *Extra*marital romance is a morale *buster*, not booster. A married boss dating an unmarried (or married) subordinate, or an unmarried boss dating a married subordinate, will offend most employees who witness it or know about it. It will also offend most *jurors*. Juries are more likely to "award" a sexual harassment victim big damages if the harasser was married than if the harasser was unmarried. In a jury's view, an unmarried supervisor is free to at least *try* to get a date or establish a romantic relationship with a subordinate—not to be *too* persistent about it, but to at least ask once. A married supervisor is not free in this regard.

Sexually Hostile Work Environment

Sexually hostile work environment refers to sexual advances, sexual conduct, or sexual comments that are so severe or so repetitious that they make it more difficult for the victim to do her job.[32] They must be that offensive in order

---

32   *Oncale v. Sundowner Offshore Services, Inc.*, 523 U.S. 75, 81 (1998) (the federal sexual harassment law "forbids only behavior so objectively offensive as to alter the 'conditions' of the victim's employment"). Ordinarily, simple teasing, offhand comments, and

to be legally classified as "sexual harassment," at least under federal law and the laws of nearly every state. And they must be "unwelcome." If the boss was not aware of the employee's displeasure with the conduct or comments, and the employee did nothing to make him aware (she didn't tell him and she didn't tell any other person of authority), and the conduct, comments, or advances were not that bad, she will probably lose.

Frequently people ask whether one sort of conduct or another comprises sexual harassment. "If I look at my secretary's legs, is that sexual harassment?" "My boss told me a dirty joke; is that sexual harassment?" "Our top customer, a 'macho man,' keeps asking our saleswoman for a date, and he always hugs her and puts his arm around her. Can she claim sexual harassment?" (This is called "third-party sexual harassment.") "Our sales clerk objects to our selling *Playboy* on the magazine rack; she claims it is sexual harassment." "Is it sexual harassment if one of our guys has the *Sports Illustrated* swimsuit calendar over his desk, or displays a picture of his girlfriend in a string bikini?" The answer is usually no. If that is all that happened—one little incident or a few little incidents—that is not sexual harassment. To be sexual harassment, the conditions have to be severe or repetitious. Grabbing a female employee's breast is severe. If it happens once, she might have a case. But the less severe the conduct, the more repetitious it has to be to amount to sexual harassment. If the conduct was not repetitious or severe, but the subordinate nonetheless complained about it and asked you to put a stop to it, and you did not put a stop to it, it might or might not be sexual harassment. It would depend on the circumstances.

Sexual objects, sexual jokes, sexual E-mail, sexual humor via Internet, sexy calendars, very sexy photographs of boyfriends, girlfriends, or strangers, and very sexual innuendoes might, if severe or repetitious enough, comprise sexual harassment.

Also, it is usually a good idea not to allow employees to wear clothing that is too revealing. Such clothing invites jokes and sexual harassment.

However, there is something you should know. Most people who sue for sexual harassment are *terminated* employees. Especially in private-sector, nonunion workplaces, it is relatively rare for an employee who is still employed by a company to sue that company for sexual harassment. Most employees

---

isolated incidents (unless extremely serious) do not amount to sexual harassment under federal law. *Clark County School District v. Breeden*, 532 U.S. 268, 270-71 (2001), citing *Faragher v. City of Boca Raton*, 524 U.S. 775, 788 (1998).

who sue for sexual harassment are employees who were fired or laid off. They are angry about getting fired or laid off, so they dredge up sexual comments and sexual incidents they heard, or claim they heard, before they were fired or laid off. They claim they objected to those comments and incidents and that their objections led to their being terminated.

Then there are employees who were not fired or laid off but claim that the harassment was so severe that they could not stand it any longer, so they quit. That is called "constructive discharge." Then there are employees who sense they are *about to* get fired or laid off, so they sue for sexual harassment hoping the employer will fear firing them or laying them off.

But rarely, at least in private-sector, nonunion workplaces, does an employee who is still working there and who is not on the verge of getting fired or laid off sue for sexual harassment.

In fact, that is true of discrimination lawsuits in general. Probably 80 percent (this is just my guess) are brought by employees who were fired or laid off. The percentage is less in government employment and unionized workplaces. That is, government employees and unionized employees *are more likely to sue an employer while still employed by that employer* than private-sector, nonunion employees are. That is because government employees and unionized employees usually feel they can sue and not get fired. They feel almost immune from getting fired. They also have many layers of grievance procedures available to them without having to pay a lawyer.

Miscellaneous Types of Sexual Harassment

As mentioned before, there are some other types of sexual harassment: *third-party sexual harassment* and *sexual favoritism*. *Third-party sexual harassment* occurs when an employee complains that someone associated with the company but not an employee of the company is sexually harassing the employee. For example, a waitress complains that a drunk customer is sexually harassing her. Employers who serve a lot of alcohol are probably more likely to be sued for "third-party" sexual harassment than those who do not.

There have been few third-party sexual harassment suits. That is because few victims of third-party sexual harassment get fired for complaining about it. A *customer* cannot *fire* your employee. As was said a few paragraphs ago, employees who sue for sexual harassment are usually *terminated* employees.

Sexual favoritism occurs when employee A is given a raise or promotion, or is retained rather than terminated in a company downsizing, because she or he is having some kind of sexual or romantic relationship with the boss. Employee B, who has the same job title and boss but is not given a raise or promotion, or is terminated in the downsizing, sues for sex discrimination. Employee B claims that employee B was discriminated against "because of sex." The law is not entirely clear on whether employee B has a case, but if employee B can prove that employee B was at least as good as, or better than, employee A, then employee B may well have a case. Sexual favoritism is a form of sexual harassment or sex discrimination.

Use your common sense and do not engage in or tolerate such types of harassment/discrimination. If you must tell your biggest customer to stop harassing your saleswoman, do so (as gently and diplomatically as possible, of course).

Finally, be aware that sexual harassment is illegal even if the harasser is harassing someone of his or her own gender.[33] It is illegal for a man to sexually harass a man, and it is illegal for a woman to sexually harass a woman.

Sexual Harassment Prevention Training is Required in Some States

Connecticut has a regulation that mandates companies with 50 or more employees to provide two hours of sexual harassment prevention training and education to all supervisors. Other states might have a similar requirement.

---

33   *Oncale v. Sundowner Offshore Services, Inc.*, 523 U.S. 75, 81 (1998).

Chapter Four

Prevent Religion Discrimination, Disability Discrimination, Age Discrimination, and Sexual Orientation Discrimination

If you are a white manager and are contemplating firing a black employee, ask yourself: "If this black employee were white and performing the job exactly as he is performing it and saying the same things and exhibiting the same attitudes and behaviors as he is in fact saying and exhibiting, would I be firing this employee?" Think hard. If your answer is yes (that is, you would fire him), then you probably can fire him. If your answer is no, then don't fire him. If your answer is no, it means race is influencing your decision.

If you are a woman contemplating firing a man, use the same type of thought process: "If this employee were a woman rather than a man, would I be firing this employee?" If your answer is yes (that is, you would fire this employee), then you probably can fire him. If your answer is no, then don't fire him. If your answer is no, it means gender is influencing your decision.

If you are 50 years old and are contemplating firing a 55 year-old employee, ask yourself: "Would I be firing this employee if he were 35 years old?" Even if you yourself are 55 years old (or older), you should, in this mental exercise, use 35 years of age rather than your own age because some people think that people their own age (and even a few years younger) are "too old" for a particular job. There are 55 year-old executives who think a 55 year-old is "too old" for some jobs.

The analysis gets a bit trickier if more than one of these traits differs from yours, but you can figure it out. If you are a 55 year-old white male contemplating firing a 50 year-old black female, ask yourself: "If this employee were a 35 year-old white male performing the job exactly as this employee is in fact performing it, and saying the same things and exhibiting the same attitudes and behaviors that this employee is in fact saying and exhibiting, would I be firing this employee?" If your honest answer is yes, then you probably can fire her.

If you suspect that the employee's being of a different *religion* or *national origin* influences you, ask yourself: "Would I be firing this employee if he were the same religion and national origin as me?" If your honest answer is yes, then you probably can fire him.

Prevent Religion Discrimination

Employers cannot discriminate against employees due to religion. Furthermore, employers are required to "reasonably accommodate" their employees' religious practices. If a Muslim woman wants to cover up her body so that only her face, hands, and feet are showing—as may be required by her religion—you probably have to allow her to do so even if it conflicts with your dress code or uniform, although it might depend on whether her religious attire (burqa, hijab, or other) poses a health or safety risk to her or others. If a Jewish employee needs to leave work at 5:00 p.m. on Friday to attend religious services or to take Saturday off completely, you probably have to allow him to. Whether you *must* allow him to do so depends on how much of a hardship it would be to you (or to your company) if he left at 5:00 p.m. Friday or took Saturday off.

You may have the right to inquire whether an employee who seeks a religious accommodation is really a follower of that religion. Some employees suddenly claim to follow a religion just so they can take a few days off or work reduced hours. If you have reason to believe that an employee who is asking you for a religion accommodation is faking his religion or exaggerating some religious requirement, you can require him to provide documentation that he really is a follower of that religion and that the religion really does have that requirement. But be careful. If you require Jews and Muslims to prove they are Jewish or Muslim but don't require Christians to prove they are Christian, that might be illegal discrimination.

What about *your* religious rights as a business owner or manager? Do you have the right to display Christmas decorations? What if a non-Christian complains about them? Would you have to take the decorations down? Can you *forbid* Christmas decorations? Can you offer Bible-study sessions? Can you *require* employees to attend them? Can you display the Ten Commandments at work? Can you require employees to attend church? Can you invite employees to attend church with you?

It is difficult to answer these questions in a short book such as this because the answers might depend on which state you are in. Different states have different legal standards pertaining to religion in the workplace. Furthermore, the answer might be very different if you are a government employer than if you are a private-sector employer. The "separation of church and state" applies to government employers but generally does not apply to private-sector employers. Therefore, private-sector employers generally have more religious freedom than government employers do.

Some general words of caution are in order, however. First, there is a difference between religious *decorations* and religious *services*. There are few if any cases in which a private-sector employer has been sued (and lost) for displaying religious decorations. If an employee were to complain, you might have to take down the decorations that are in that employee's immediate work area. If employees of other religions wish to display their own religious decorations at their own workstations, you probably have to let them.

As for religious *services* (prayer services), you probably have the right to *offer* them but not the right to *compel* employees to attend. You cannot punish or discriminate against employees who do not attend. And keep this in mind: Employers who conduct or offer prayer services in the workplace are almost inviting employee lawsuits even if the employees have little chance of winning these suits. If an employee is fired, not promoted, or not hired, he or she will likely claim to be a victim of religious discrimination. He or she will claim that the employer prefers to hire, promote, and retain people of a certain religion. Employers who conduct or offer religious activities in the workplace probably do prefer employees who are of the employer's religion. While it is legal to express your religious views, it is illegal to discriminate against employees because their religious views differ from yours. So be careful. Be especially careful if the religion your company or organization espouses is not a mainstream religion. A jury might be less likely to sympathize with your company or organization.

If your company or organization serves a particular religious purpose (for example, if it is a church, synagogue, or mosque), the rules are somewhat different. Only members of your religion may be qualified to hold certain jobs. Religion may be a *bona fide occupational qualification* (BFOQ) for certain jobs. But other jobs can be held by members of any religion, and you do not have the right to discriminate on the basis of religion when hiring, promoting, and retaining people for these other jobs.

Prevent Disability Discrimination

If an employee has a disability but it does not affect his or her job performance, or affects it in a minor way, ask yourself: "Would I be firing this disabled employee if he or she were not disabled?" If your answer is yes—you would be firing the employee if he or she were not disabled—you can, ordinarily (except in some unusual circumstances), fire the employee and not be held liable for disability discrimination (and hopefully not even get sued).

However, some disabilities do affect job performance. Some disabilities make it very difficult or impossible to perform certain jobs. That is why they are called *disabilities*. Therefore, the analysis in a disability discrimination case is often more complicated than it is in a race, age, gender, or religion discrimination case. The laws prohibiting race, age, gender, and religion discrimination are based on the assumption that race, age, gender, and religion have *no* effect on job performance. The laws prohibiting disability discrimination, on the other hand, are based on the assumption that many disabilities do affect job performance. In fact, some disabilities make job performance *very difficult* or *impossible*. If the disability makes the person unable to do the job, you generally do not have to hire or retain that person.

However, disability discrimination law also assumes that (1) *not all* disabilities affect job performance, (2) a particular disability might affect the job performance of *some* employees who have that disability but not *other* employees who have that disability, and (3) even if a disability does make it difficult or impossible for an employee to do the job, there may exist some type of inexpensive mechanism or accommodation that enables that employee to do the job as well as the employer's "abled" (the opposite of *dis*abled) employees do. Consequently, if there exists such a mechanism or accommodation, the employer is required to provide it. If there does not exist such a mechanism or accommodation and the disabled employee simply cannot perform the job as well as the employer's "abled" employees do, the employer need not hire or retain that disabled employee.

In other words, disability discrimination law protects people who *can do the job.* Those who cannot do the job even with whatever mechanisms or accommodations are reasonably available are not protected by the disability discrimination laws. You do not have to hire or retain them.

Thus, employers should not have a *stereotypical* view of disabilities. For example, an employer should not *assume,* just because an employee suffers from depression (which is usually a "disability" under the Americans with Disabilities Act, or ADA), that the employee's job performance will be less than that of employees who do not suffer from depression. It might or might not be less. With most disabilities, employers should look at the disabled employee as an individual who may or may not have the same work problems as someone else with that disability.

Here are the general principles of disability discrimination law: If an employee's disability prevents the employee from performing the essential functions of the job in accordance with your company's standards (that is, prevents him from performing them as well as your "abled" employees perform them), you can terminate him; however, you first must consider whether there exists some mechanism or accommodation that might enable him to perform up to those standards. If such a mechanism or accommodation exists and you can provide it without undue hardship (financial or other type of hardship) to your company, you must provide it.

You can require the employee to pay that part of the cost of the accommodation that is an undue hardship to your company.[34] However,

---

34   "Reasonable Accommodation and Undue Hardship under the Americans with Disabilities Act," EEOC Enforcement Guidance, Oct. 17, 2002 ("Undue Hardship Issues"), http://www.eeoc.gov/policy/docs/accommodation.html (last visited Mar. 14, 2013).

you must first try to determine whether tax credits or deductions might offset the cost of the accommodation, and also explore whether funding might be available from an outside source, such as a state rehabilitation agency.

These requirements are called *reasonable accommodation*. If no reasonably affordable mechanism or accommodation exists that will enable the employee to perform up to your company's standards, then you need not hire or retain that employee. For example, if your company requires all its clerical people to be able to type at least 70 words per minute accurately, and a disabled employee or job applicant cannot type more than 50 words per minute accurately even with whatever accommodations or mechanisms could reasonably be provided to him or her, you need not hire or retain that employee/job applicant.[35]

The important point to remember is that you do not have to tolerate lesser productivity from a disabled employee than you do from an employee with no disability. You can tolerate lesser productivity if you want to, but you don't have to. Disabled employees can be held to the same standards as abled workers. An employer need not evaluate disabled employees by a lower standard.[36] However, you do have to explore whether a lesser-performing disabled employee might be able to perform as well as your abled employees if he or she is provided with some type of reasonably inexpensive mechanism or accommodation.

You have to be careful in the job-interviewing process not to ask employees if they have disabilities or to question them about disabilities. You can tell them what the various aspects of the job are and you can ask them if they can perform the various aspects of the job and to demonstrate that they can. Asking them to submit to a medical examination or to provide medical documentation is sometimes permitted in the hiring process.

---

35 See U.S. Equal Employment Opportunity Commission, "The Americans With Disabilities Act: Applying Performance And Conduct Standards To Employees With Disabilities," http://www.eeoc.gov/facts/performance-conduct.html (last visited Mar. 14, 2013). This particular document on the EEOC's website is excellent and I highly recommend that employers read it.

36 This is according to footnote 17 of "The Americans With Disabilities Act: Applying Performance And Conduct Standards To Employees With Disabilities" on the EEOC's website, http://www.eeoc.gov/facts/performance-conduct.html (last visited Mar. 14, 2013).

Asking current employees (as opposed to job applicants) to submit to a medical examination is permitted if job related and consistent with business necessity.[37]

What types of accommodations might you have to provide a disabled employee to enable him or her to perform the essential functions of a particular job in accordance with company standards? There are manuals on this topic and thus no need to list them all here. Most are a matter of common sense. One accommodation you may have to provide is sick time and light duty. You may have to provide extra sick days (in most cases, the extra sick days can be unpaid), light duty, a leave of absence, or some scheduling flexibility to an employee to accommodate his or her disability. At some point, however, if the employee is absent too much, the employee will no longer be considered a "qualified individual" under the disability discrimination laws. In essence, he will no longer be regarded as "qualified" for the job, and thus can be legally terminated.

Disability discrimination law can be rather tricky and difficult to explain in a short book and, like all types of discrimination, the answers to specific questions often depend on which state you are in. Generally speaking, though, common sense and decency will suffice to keep employers out of trouble and cost them very little or nothing. Employers can easily comply with the disability discrimination laws without giving up anything in productivity or discipline.

The legal definition of disability under the Americans with Disabilities Act ("ADA") is rather vague: "a physical or mental impairment that substantially limits one or more of the major life activities of [the employee]." "Major life activities" include, for example, caring for oneself, performing manual tasks, seeing, hearing, eating, sleeping, walking, standing, lifting, bending, speaking, breathing, learning, reading, concentrating, thinking, communicating, and working. "Major life activities" also include the operation of a major bodily function, for example, functions of the immune system, normal cell growth, digestive, bowel, bladder, neurological, brain,

---

37 "Disability-Related Inquiries and Medical Examinations of Employees under the Americans with Disabilities Act," EEOC Enforcement Guidance, July 27, 2000, http://www.eeoc.gov/policy/docs/guidance-inquiries.htm (last visited Mar. 15, 2013); 42 U.S.C. §12102(2)(A); see also "Questions and Answers: Enforcement Guidance on Disability-Related Inquiries and Medical Examinations of Employees under the Americans with Disabilities Act," http://www.eeoc.gov/policy/docs/qanda-inquiries.html (last visited Mar. 14, 2013).

respiratory, circulatory, endocrine, and reproductive functions.[38] Congress and the EEOC recently made it easier for employees to establish they have a disability. Congress passed the ADA Amendments Act of 2008 (ADAAA). On March 25, 2011, the EEOC issued regulations interpreting the ADAAA. The EEOC declared:

> The primary purpose of the ADAAA is to make it easier for people with disabilities to obtain protection under the ADA. Consistent with the Amendments Act's purpose of reinstating a broad scope of protection under the ADA, the definition of "disability" in this part shall be construed broadly in favor of expansive coverage to the maximum extent permitted by the terms of the ADA. The primary object of attention in cases brought under the ADA should be whether covered entities have complied with their obligations and whether discrimination has occurred, not whether the individual meets the definition of disability. The question of whether an individual meets the definition of disability under this part should not demand extensive analysis.
>
> . . ..
>
> For example, . . .it should easily be concluded that the following types of impairments will, at a minimum, substantially limit the major life activities indicated: Deafness substantially limits hearing; blindness substantially limits seeing; an intellectual disability (formerly termed mental retardation) substantially limits brain function; partially or completely missing limbs or mobility impairments requiring the use of a wheelchair substantially limit musculoskeletal function; autism substantially limits brain function; cancer substantially limits normal cell growth; cerebral palsy substantially limits brain function; diabetes substantially limits endocrine function; epilepsy substantially limits neurological function; Human Immunodeficiency Virus (HIV) infection substantially limits immune function;

---

38   42 U.S.C. §§ 12102(1)(A) & 12102(2).

> multiple sclerosis substantially limits neurological function; muscular dystrophy substantially limits neurological function; and major depressive disorder, bipolar disorder, post-traumatic stress disorder, obsessive compulsive disorder, and schizophrenia substantially limit brain function. The types of impairments described in this section may substantially limit additional major life activities not explicitly listed above.

In other words, the EEOC goes on to say, "disability" includes, *for example* (these are just examples) deafness, blindness, intellectual disability (formerly known as mental retardation), partially or completely missing limbs, mobility impairments requiring use of a wheelchair, autism, cancer, cerebral palsy, diabetes, epilepsy, HIV infection, multiple sclerosis, muscular dystrophy, major depressive disorder, bipolar disorder, post-traumatic stress disorder, obsessive-compulsive disorder, schizophrenia, any mental or psychological disorder, organic brain syndrome, emotional or mental illness, and specific learning disabilities."[39]

But this recent development should not alarm employers. Many millions of employees in the U.S. can prove they have some type of disability, according to the ADAAA and EEOC. This does not necessarily mean they can win a disability discrimination lawsuit. It merely means that the employer's focus should be on whether the employer is complying with the law rather than on whether the employee qualifies as being "disabled." Courts rarely require employers to put up with a disabled employee's job performance if that job performance falls short of the job performance of the other employees (the employees who have no disability),[40] so long as the employer makes a reasonable effort to help the employee perform up to the standards set for employees who have no disability. Just having a disability doesn't get an employee very far in a disability discrimination lawsuit. The employee must also prove *discrimination* or *failure to reasonably accommodate a disability.* Failure to reasonably accommodate a disability is a form of disability discrimination, according to the ADA.

Put another way, the mere fact that an employee is *disabled* does not help him win an ADA lawsuit any more than the fact that an employee is black

---

39   http://www.eeoc.gov/laws/regulations/ada_qa_final_rule.cfm (last visited Aug. 28, 2012).

40   See note 35 on page 54.

helps him (the black employee) win a race discrimination lawsuit. The key question, as to the black employee, should be not whether he is black but whether the employer is discriminating against him because he is black. Likewise, the key question as to the disabled employee should be whether the employer is discriminating against him because of his disability (or failing to reasonably accommodate the disability).

An employee also has a "disability" under the ADA if he has a "record of such an impairment" or is "regarded as having such an impairment."[41] For example, an employee who was committed to a mental hospital 10 years ago might be "regarded" by some people as still mentally impaired today even if he has a "clean bill of health" today. He also has a "record of such an impairment."

Short-term illnesses and short-term injuries (minor illnesses and injuries lasting or expected to last less than six months) are usually not "disabilities" under the ADA, though it might depend on circumstances. Pregnancy is not a "disability" (it is not an "impairment"), but certain impairments resulting from pregnancy (e.g., gestational diabetes) may be considered a disability if they substantially limit a major life activity.

I encourage you to become familiar with the U.S. Equal Employment Opportunity Commission's website and the website of your state agency that has jurisdiction over employment discrimination claims. The EEOC's website, in particular, has a lot of helpful information, including information pertinent to specific disabilities such as cancer, diabetes, deafness (and other hearing impairments), blindness (and other vision impairments), and other disabilities, and also information pertinent to some specific types of employers, such as restaurants, other food service providers, and some other specific types of employers.

If an employee claims to have a condition that is a disability and asks that you accommodate it, and you are not sure whether the employee really does have that condition, ordinarily you have the right to ask the employee to furnish medical proof that he has this condition. This is particularly true of non-obvious ("invisible") disabilities such as mental disabilities, headaches, depression, learning disabilities, certain types of back pain, and other disabilities that an employee can fake or exaggerate. Just because an employee claims he has one of these conditions does not mean the employer has to take the employee's word for it. The employer can ask the employee

---

41 42 U.S.C. § 12102(1)(B) & (C).

to produce medical records to show he has this condition. If the employee refuses to produce the records or if the records do not indicate that he has this condition, the employee must somehow prove to the employer that he has the condition. If he doesn't, the employer need not provide the accommodation.[42] Disability, like religion, is often invisible. That means it can be faked or exaggerated. Employers have a right to ascertain whether the employee is faking or exaggerating it.

Prevent Age Discrimination

Many people misunderstand age discrimination law. They think age discrimination law makes it illegal to terminate older workers. Or they think employers have to allow older workers to slow down and be less productive than younger workers.

They are mistaken. Older workers can be terminated just as younger workers can. If an older worker is unable to perform the job as well as all your younger workers do, you can terminate him. This is true even if his inability is due to the effects of aging. You are thereby terminating him not because of age, but because of job performance.

If, on the other hand, he *is* able to perform the job as well as your younger workers, you must treat him no differently than you treat them.

Basically, the law requires you to make an assumption: that age, if 40 or older (but in Connecticut and perhaps a few other states, any age that is old enough to be hired for the job), has no effect on job performance.[43] But obviously that assumption is not always correct. Some workers, especially in highly physical occupations, become less effective at their jobs as they get older. For example, in March 2013 there is no one, to my knowledge (correct me if I'm mistaken) over the age of 46 playing in the National Football League, Major League Baseball, the National Basketball Association, or the National Hockey League. Only a handful are over 40. Hundreds of major-

---

42 ADA regulation 29 CFR §1630.9 (App.): "When the need for accommodation is not obvious, an employer, before providing a reasonable accommodation, may require that the individual with a disability provide documentation of the need for accommodation."

43 See *EEOC v. Wyoming*, 460 U.S. 226, 231 (1983) (pointing out that the U.S. Secretary of Labor conducted a study that found that, generally speaking, the job performance of older workers is at least as good as that of younger workers).

league athletes in their early 40s are "cut from the team" (terminated) each year and replaced with younger athletes. The diminished ability of the older athletes is due to the effects of aging and the general wear and tear that eventually takes a toll on a major-league athlete.

If older athletes are cut from the team due to their diminished ability, does that mean they are victims of *age discrimination*? No. They were terminated not because of age but because of job performance. True, their job performance declined due to age. But they were terminated due to job performance, not age. If a 22 year-old were performing no better than these 42 year-olds, he would be terminated, too.

From his late teens until his early 40s, baseball pitcher Roger Clemens could throw a baseball 98 miles per hour, which is very fast. After he reached the age of about 43 (in 2007), his fastball slowed a bit. He retired from baseball. In August 2012, at the age of 50, he tried to make a comeback, or at least appeared to try to make a comeback. He pitched for a minor-league baseball team. He threw only about 87 miles per hour in 2012, which is not high by Major League standards. If a Major League team refuses to hire Clemens because Clemens can throw no faster than 87 miles per hour, is that age discrimination? The answer is no. Age, or the effect of aging, has caused Clemens to be unable to throw faster than about 87 miles per hour. But if he is rejected for a pitching job, it is not "because of" his age. It is "because" he cannot throw faster than 87 miles per hour. If a 22-year-old pitcher were unable to pitch faster than 87 miles per hour, he too would probably be rejected by Major League teams. The rejection is "because of" his pitching speed (or lack thereof), not his age.[44] Suppose, however, that Clemens keeps trying to improve his pitching speed and that he eventually, in 2013, is throwing 96 miles per hour. If a team rejects him at age 51 because the team simply *assumes, due to his age,* that Clemens will be unable to continue to throw 96 miles per hour, *that would be age discrimination.*

That is what I mean when I say age discrimination law is about *assumptions.* Remember what I said about gender discrimination: don't *assume,* just because

---

44 I am well aware that Clemens was indicted for lying to Congress about steroid use. But he went to trial,, and the jury found him not guilty. So the steroids controversy, in my opinion, is irrelevant to my illustration of how the age discrimination laws work. I am using Clemens to illustrate how the age discrimination laws work.

a 150-pound person is female, that she cannot perform a job as well as a 150-pound man. Maybe she can, maybe she can't. Don't make assumptions just because she is female and he is male. Get the facts. It may well be that that particular woman cannot perform the job as well as that particular man. But don't just *assume* it because she is female.

So too with age discrimination. Don't assume, just because an employee is older, that he is unable to perform as well as younger employees perform. Don't assume that older workers ("older" being defined in federal age discrimination law and in most states' age discrimination laws as *40 or older*) are physically or mentally slower, more apt to retire, or more apt to get sick or die soon, than younger workers are. Some are, some aren't. Ordinarily (there might be an occasional exception to this), you should not ask an employee if, or when, the employee plans to retire, unless the employee mentions it first, and even then you should try to focus the discussion on the employee's plans, not the employee's age.

However, if for whatever reason, including age, an employee cannot perform as well as your younger employees perform, you need not retain that employee. As with handicap discrimination law, if age has caused the employee to be less effective than your other employees, you can terminate that employee. You can terminate an employee for being less effective than your other employees. So focus on *job performance* and *ignore age*. That is easy in baseball because baseball performance is easily measured in numbers. The speed of Roger Clemens's fastball was easily measured by a machine. A pitcher's overall job performance is easily measured by familiar (to baseball fans) statistics such as his "earned run average," strikeouts, and win-loss record. But in most other types of jobs, performance is not so easily measured. When performance is difficult to measure, managers are more apt to consider age.

Managers should not do that. Managers should ignore age. How do you *ignore* age? Easy. When contemplating terminating an older worker, pretend the worker has a full head of hair (and the same *color* hair the employee had when young), unwrinkled skin, and all other outward appearances of youth. Pretend you have no idea how old the worker is. Then ask yourself: "Is this worker performing as well as my younger workers?" If he or she is not—in other words, if his or her job performance is worse than that of *all* your younger workers in the same job category and perhaps some similar job categories—you can terminate this older worker. But if even *one* younger worker is a worse performer than the older (40 or older) worker, *reconsider* whom to terminate. Perhaps you should terminate the *younger* one, or maybe *both* of them. Visualize, in your mind, Roger Clemens on the pitcher's mound in 2013. He is 51 years old, but you should completely ignore his age. You should focus solely on his pitching speed and other aspects of his pitching ability. Pretend he is 25 years old. If a 25-year-old were pitching the way (speed, quality, and other measures of good baseball pitching) Clemens is pitching, would you hire the 25-year-old. If your answer is no, then you do not have to hire Clemens. Your answer is based solely on pitching ability, not age.

If it helps, here is a little song, or rhyme, you can remember. It is sung to the tune of "This Old Man":

> This old man,
> he can sue;
> I'll pretend he's thirty-two.[45]

In other words, if you are contemplating terminating an older worker, pretend that a 32 year-old worker (a worker who is 32 and looks 32) were performing the job with the same speed and effectiveness that this older worker is performing it. Would you fire the 32 year-old? If your answer is yes—you would fire the 32 year-old worker—then you can probably fire the older worker. If your answer is no—you would not fire the 32 year-old—then don't fire the older worker. If your answer is no, it means that the employee's *age*, not his *job performance*, is influencing your thinking. When his age, not job performance, is influencing your thinking, that is age discrimination and is generally illegal.

Having a workplace that reflects the age of the general population (or is *above* the age of the general population) reduces your likelihood of being accused of age discrimination. In all but a few states, it is legal to discriminate in favor of an older worker or older job applicant and against a younger one. Thus, in all but a few states, it might be a good idea, in order to make sure you have a good number of older workers, to discriminate

---

45 I made up this little rhyme for an article I wrote twenty years ago. See David A. Robinson, "Age Discrimination: A Short Guide and a Practical Tip," published in *Chamber Channels*, the newsletter of Affiliated Chambers of Commerce of Greater Springfield, Mass., in June 1992.

(not a lot, but a little) in favor of older workers over younger workers in the hiring and retention process. In all but a few states, discrimination *in favor of* older workers is legal. Discrimination *against* older workers is illegal in all states, although the age discrimination laws do make exceptions for a few types of jobs.

Tips to Help Prevent Becoming a Victim of Age Discrimination

What can older workers do to prevent being discriminated against? Three things: exercise, education, and mentoring. Exercise enables older workers to stay in good physical shape and avoid getting overweight. Physically fit older workers are far less likely to be discriminated against than physically unfit ones are. You don't have to dye your hair or tattoo your body. You can "look your age." But try to look as good for your age as you possibly can. Make it your *skills* that stand out—not your age.[46]

Older workers should consider taking college courses and other *continuing education* courses. This demonstrates their willingness and ability to learn and change. It is sad to read about older workers being downsized out of jobs they have held for many years. But whose fault is it? Is it the fault of the employer, or is it the fault of the employee? Some employees get complacent as they get older, do not maintain their skills and good attitude, and do not learn new skills. When they get fired, they think it is because of their age. Sometimes they are right. But more often it is because they *got complacent, did not maintain their skills and good attitude,* and *did not learn new skills.* In those situations, the firing is not age discrimination. Such employees would have been fired even if they were 25 years old.

Older workers should mentor younger workers and help younger workers succeed. If you help a younger worker and she later becomes a CEO, and you need a job someday, maybe she will return the favor and hire you.

One problem for many older workers is they become too dependent on *one* employer—*their* employer. If that employer terminates them, they are devastated. They fear they will not be able to find a job elsewhere at their age. But again, whose fault is that? The employer's? Or their own?

---

46   The sentence "Make it your skills that stand out—not your age" appeared in a *Boston Sunday Globe* (July 29, 2001, at H10) calendar of upcoming lectures and workshops, pertaining to a workshop for older job seekers.

Employees should maintain *employability*, so that if an employer fires them or lays them off, they can go out and find another job without too much difficulty. Employers should encourage employees to maintain employability. Employers should encourage employees to maintain their skills, learn new skills, and learn new technology. Getting dumped by an employer is like getting dumped by a girlfriend or boyfriend: painful though it is, the pain goes away as soon as the dumped one finds another (satisfactory) girlfriend or boyfriend. An employee who quickly finds another job is less likely to sue you than one who suffers a long period of unemployment.

Note that I use a *boyfriend* or *girlfriend* analogy, not a *marriage* analogy. Some employees are as devastated by losing a job as they would be if their spouse died or divorced them. They have no right to feel this way. They were not "married" to the employer. Few, if any, of them had a lifetime contract with the employer, as husbands and wives have with each other. They were, in most cases, employees-at-will, meaning, according to the laws of most states, they had the right to quit at any time without explanation, and the employer had the right to terminate them at any time without explanation (so long as the employer was not motivated by the employee's race, color, national origin, gender, or other illegal reason). They should simply move on and find a new employer. Employers should help them prepare for this possibility by encouraging them to keep themselves in good vocational shape so they are attractive to other employers.

Here is a story that illustrates the point.

The Story of the Boyfriends and the Girlfriends

Two men had attractive girlfriends ("girlfriend" and "boyfriend" are acceptable words to refer to romantic companions even if the "girl" and "boy" are both well over 18; this is an exception to the "rule" that says men should not refer to women over 18 as "girls"). The first man got complacent about the relationship and gained 50 pounds of flab. When his girlfriend dumped him without explanation, he felt hurt. But the hurt intensified when he found that he was unable, due to being so out of shape, to land another attractive woman. So he kept trying to win back the girlfriend, which made him (and her) even more miserable. He became a nuisance to her.

The second man also got dumped without explanation, but he had stayed strong and fit, so he easily found another attractive woman to date and quickly forgot about the woman who dumped him. In fact, the woman who dumped him eventually got jealous and tried to win him back, without success.

The moral of the story is, an employee who stays "in shape" is less likely to bother (sue) an employer if the employer "dumps" (fires) him. He'll find another job easily. This is true even if he is an older employee. Although some employers discriminate against older employees, many do not. Many *prefer* older employees.

So encourage your employees to stay in good vocational "shape." If you eventually fire them or lay them off, they will find new jobs quickly and be less likely to try to drag you down with them. Furthermore, you might just decide not to fire them or lay them off. An "in shape" employee is one you won't want to lose!

Prevent Sexual Orientation Discrimination (at Least in Those States in Which Sexual Orientation Discrimination is Illegal)

If you are an employer in one of the seventeen (or so) states, or the District of Columbia, that prohibit discrimination based on sexual orientation, and you know, or think, that an employee or job applicant is gay, lesbian, or bisexual, and you are contemplating firing, demoting, denying a promotion to, or not hiring this employee or job applicant, ask yourself: What if this employee or applicant were heterosexual? Would you be taking such action? If your answer is yes, then you can probably fire, demote, not promote, or not hire this employee or applicant. But if your answer is no, then don't take such action.

From a lawsuit prevention standpoint, it is better, in those seventeen states and D.C., that you *not* know who is gay and who is not. If you do not know, and you do not think, an employee is gay, it will be difficult for the employee to accuse you of sexual orientation discrimination. The less you know about their sexual orientation, the better. Whether that is a good way, or not, to deal with your employees, it is probably the best strategy in those 17 states to prevent sexual orientation discrimination lawsuits.

Some employees who sue for sexual orientation discrimination are not gay, lesbian, or bisexual. They are, or claim to be, heterosexual. What are they suing for, then? They are suing based on what is called "perceived" homosexuality. The boss referred to the employee by using a word or name—derogatory or neutral—that means or implies that the employee is gay, lesbian, or bisexual. In some states, if an employee is fired or otherwise treated less favorably because the employer believed or perceived him or her to be gay, lesbian, or bisexual, or somehow identified him or her as gay, lesbian, or bisexual, the employee can sue for sexual orientation discrimination even if the employee is not gay, lesbian, or bisexual.

Many people refer to the lesbian, gay, and bisexual community as the LGBT community. "T" stands for "transgendered." "Transgendered" includes, for example, men who dress like women and wear women's makeup and lipstick, and includes people who undergo sex-change operations. In a state where sexual orientation discrimination is illegal, can an employer fire a male employee because he wears a dress or skirt to work, or because he underwent a sex-change operation and now looks and sounds, or tries to look and sound, like a woman? The answer depends on the circumstances. In Connecticut, it is illegal to discriminate against an employee because of the employee's "gender identity or expression." In Connecticut, "gender identity or expression" means:

> a person's gender-related identity, appearance or
> behavior, whether or not that gender-related identity,
> appearance or behavior is different from that traditionally
> associated with the person's physiology or assigned sex
> at birth, which gender-related identity can be shown by
> providing evidence including, but not limited to, medical
> history, care or treatment of the gender-related identity,
> consistent and uniform assertion of the gender-related
> identity or any other evidence that the gender-related
> identity is sincerely held, part of a person's core identity
> or not being asserted for an improper purpose.[47]

Suppose you are a Connecticut employer and one of your male employees is doing his job poorly. You've given him a final warning. He, in a last-ditch effort to either save his job or ensure, if you fire him, that he has a strong lawsuit against you, shows up for work the next day wearing a dress. Can you fire him? Can you, at the very least, send him home and tell him he can

---

47   Conn. General Statutes § 46a-51(21).

return to work only if he takes off the dress and puts pants on? The answers (in Connecticut) are not entirely clear. The employee will claim he was fired for wearing a dress. He'll argue that the employer thus discriminated against him on the basis of gender identity or expression. Will the employee win the suit? The employee will have to prove that he "sincerely" (note the word "sincerely" in the statute above) identifies more with the female gender than the male gender. If he has never been treated for gender identity disorder and never before asserted his "femininity," he will have difficulty proving his sudden assertion of his femininity is "sincere."

But this law nonetheless causes uncertainty for the employer. What previously was clear—an employer could fire a male employee, or at least send him home to change his clothes, for wearing a dress to work—is now unclear in Connecticut. Many LGBT people and their supporters are trying, by political lobbying and litigation, to persuade lawmakers to prohibit employers from discriminating against "transgendered" or cross-dressing employees. They want employers to be required by law to treat transgendered employees and job applicants as favorably as other employees and job applicants and required by law to allow male employees to wear dresses, skirts, makeup, and other attire traditionally worn by women. Employers who are concerned about this should monitor developments in the law (federal law and the law of their particular state) regarding transgendered or cross-dressing employees and job applicants.

In any sexual orientation discrimination case, the employee will likely have to answer some very personal, and perhaps embarrassing, questions to prove that he really is, or really is perceived by others to be, homosexual or bisexual. Furthermore, the employee's sexual orientation might have changed at some point. Some people are gay their entire lives (by "entire lives," I mean beginning at whatever age they develop sexual feelings). Some people are heterosexual their entire lives. Some people are somewhere in between. Some people are heterosexual their entire lives except they are physically attracted to one or two people of their own gender at some point during their lives. Some of these basically heterosexual people will have sex with these one or two people of their own gender. Some will not. Some people are gay their entire lives except they are physically attracted to one or two people of the opposite sex at some point in their lives. Some will have sex with those people. Some will not. Some might even marry one of those people. Some women are physically attracted to, and have sex with, and even marry, effeminate men. Some men are physically attracted to, and have sex with, and even marry, masculine women.

What labels shall we use for such people? "Gay?" "Straight?" "Heterosexual?" "Homosexual?" "Bisexual?" Here is a suggestion, a suggestion that might help prevent sexual orientation discrimination in the workplace: Let us not label sexual orientation at all. Such labels classify people in a way that does not necessarily reflect who they are, who they were, or who they might become. It is okay to call ("label") a man "Mr." or "he" and a woman "Ms.," "Miss," "Mrs.," or "her." It is okay to provide separate restrooms for men and women. It is okay to have separate dress codes for men and women, although in those few states where transgender discrimination is illegal, you might have to accommodate an employee's sincere desire to dress like the opposite gender (see pages 66-67). But otherwise you should not try to *label*, even in your mind, your employees' sexual orientation.

The employer's defense in a sexual orientation discrimination suit is often, "I had no idea he is gay. I fired him because of his poor job performance, not his sexual orientation. I didn't know what his sexual orientation is." If the employer is telling the truth, it will be very difficult for the employee to win the suit. If the employee never clearly indicated to the employer that the employee is gay, lesbian, or bisexual, the employee will have difficulty proving that the employer "knew" or "perceived" the employee to be gay, lesbian, or bisexual. If the employer did not know or perceive it, the employer could not possibly have discriminated against the employee on the basis of it.

For that reason, diversity training pertaining to sexual orientation is inadvisable. That type of diversity training makes almost everyone feel uncomfortable. It generates discussion about a topic that many people have strong feelings about but would rather not discuss in the workplace. Negative feelings, if expressed, can be used against them and against the company in court. The more interest and curiosity you show in an employee's sexual orientation (some diversity trainers urge managers to show such interest in their employees), the more legal trouble you potentially bring upon yourself and your company or organization. A gay, lesbian, or bisexual employee might accuse you of prying into his or her love life because you are "homophobic" and you are trying to "get rid of" homosexual employees. Keep in mind that you cannot please everybody (see page 15 above). If an employee or diversity trainer is displeased because you do not wish to talk about sexual orientation in the workplace, keep in mind that your first obligation is to *comply with the law.* In the (approximately) seventeen states that prohibit sexual orientation discrimination in the workplace, the best way to comply with the law is to *ignore* the sexual orientation of your employees.

Suppose you are an employer in one of the (approximately) seventeen states that prohibit sexual orientation discrimination, and you disapprove of homosexuality. Can you express your disapproval to your employees? My answer to that question is basically the same as the answer I gave previously in this chapter about a somewhat related topic, *religion.* You probably have the right to politely (that is, not in a harassing or threatening way) express your disapproval of homosexuality to your employees, but if you do express your disapproval of homosexuality to your employees, you significantly increase the risk, if you fire an employee who is gay, lesbian, or bisexual, of being accused of sexual orientation discrimination. Thus, you have rights, including the First Amendment right of freedom of speech to express your views, but your employees also have rights, including the right not to be discriminated against or harassed on the basis of sexual orientation. Sometimes rights clash, and it is difficult to predict whether a court will balance those rights in *your* favor or in *your employee's* favor. The safest legal advice in these seventeen states and D.C. is to *ignore* your employees' homosexuality (if any) and not express your disapproval (if any) of homosexuality to your employees.

What about the other 33 (or so) states? In the 33 (or so) states that do not have a state law prohibiting sexual orientation discrimination, can an employer fire, or refuse to hire, an employee for being lesbian, gay, bisexual, or transgendered? Until Obama became President, the answer to that question was yes. Has that changed since he became President? The answer is somewhere between yes and no. As of this writing (March 2013), the federal statutes pertaining to employment discrimination in the private sector have changed little, if at all, under Obama. However, Obama is trying to persuade courts to interpret the word "sex" in Title VII of the Civil Rights Act of 1964—the federal law that make various types of discrimination, including "sex" discrimination, illegal if an employer has fifteen or more employees (see page 9)—to mean more than simply the gender of the employee. The Obama Administration wants courts to interpret the word "sex" in that statute to also mean the gender of people the employee has sex with. Whether the Administration will succeed in persuading courts to do so is difficult to predict. Employers who are concerned about this should monitor developments in this regard and tell their lawmakers what the concerns are.

Prevent Genetics Discrimination

Under federal law and the laws of some states, it is illegal to discriminate against an employee (or job applicant) because of his or her genetics or family medical history. This is a fairly new development in employment discrimination law, although it is, in some ways, simply an extension of the laws that prohibit discrimination based on ancestry and gender. For more information, see the EEOC's GINA (Genetic Information Nondiscrimination Act) regulations[48] and your state's regulations.

Post All Required Notices and Undergo Any Required Training

Federal and state employment laws require employers to display certain posters telling employees what their rights are. Make sure you display all such posters—properly. Failure to display them properly can be used against you in court.

---

48   29 CFR (Code of Federal Regulations) § 1635; see also http://www.eeoc.gov/laws/types/genetic.cfm (last visited Mar. 14, 2013).

Chapter Five

Prevent Discriminatory Language

Eliminate from your vocabulary, especially your workplace vocabulary, all offensive words that pertain to race, color, ethnicity, ancestry, national origin, gender, pregnancy, religion, old age, physical or mental disability, and sexual orientation. If a jury hears that you uttered discriminatory slurs, the jury might conclude that you committed employment discrimination even if you did not commit employment discrimination. Also, such words might constitute racial *harassment*, ethnicity *harassment*, national origin *harassment*, gender *harassment*, age *harassment*, disability *harassment*, genetics *harassment*, or sexual orientation *harassment*. *Harassment* based on one or more of those categories is a form of *discrimination* based on one or more of those categories. Here is a story that illustrates the point:

The Story of the Latino Factory Worker

A Latino male (we'll refer to him as "the client") went to a lawyer complaining that the client's boss, Mr. Smith—a gruff, white, semi-educated factory owner—used an ethnic slur to refer to Latinos and fired him for being late too often. Although the client was indeed late too often, he wanted to sue for race discrimination or ethnicity discrimination. He felt that if a white employee had been late that often, Smith would have given the white employee one more chance to improve his punctuality, rather than fire him.

The lawyer asked the client how many of Smith's 100 employees are Latino. The client replied 50. The lawyer advised the client that he (the client) might have a good race discrimination case or ethnicity discrimination case, and suggested in passing that he go to work for the competing factory about a mile away.

The competing factory was owned by Mr. Jones, a dignified white man with an Ivy League education who is on many civic boards, goes to church every Sunday, and never utters a slur of any type. The client's reply to the lawyer's suggestion was, "I don't think I can get a job there. Jones does not hire Latinos. He does not like Latinos. So I want to sue Smith to get my job back."

Who's the bigot, Smith or Jones? Ordinarily, *actions* speak louder than *words*. Smith's *actions* show him to be an equal opportunity employer—half of his employees are Latino. Jones has no Latino employees (or he has a few "tokens" just to avoid being accused of having an all-white workforce). Jones is the bigot. Smith might be *somewhat* bigoted, but Jones is a worse bigot.

But who does the client wish to sue? Smith! Why? Because Smith used an ethnic slur and fired him. He does not wish to sue Jones even though Jones is more bigoted than Smith and even though Jones would have refused to hire the client at all. In employment discrimination law, *words* often speak louder than actions.

Jones will probably get sued eventually. An employer should not try to avoid discrimination suits by simply refusing to hire women, people of color, older workers, and disabled workers. That is illegal. But that isn't the point here. The point here is that some of the most fair-minded employers—the ones who hire the most women and people of color—end up getting sued because they make *offensive, discriminatory* remarks. Don't make such remarks! Discriminatory remarks can get an employer into trouble even if the employer has a good or even excellent record of hiring women, people of color, older workers, and disabled workers.

Remember also that some people who would never utter a discriminatory slur under ordinary circumstances might do so in *extra*ordinary circumstances, such as when they are *extremely agitated*. Maybe you are one of them. A white worker, in a heated argument with a black co-worker, yells a racial epithet at the black co-worker. Or a young worker will call an older worker an "old" this or that. Or a male manager will call a female employee a gender-specific slur. Make a conscious effort to "catch yourself" when you're angry, so you do not utter such slurs.

And don't allow any *other* employee of yours—even your lowest-level employee—to make such remarks in the workplace. Such remarks create a discriminatorily hostile work environment.

I considered making a list of all these discriminatory slurs, or as many as I could think of, and including the list in this book so you would know all the words to avoid. Some people do not know that all these words are offensive. But the list would be too offensive to put in the book. So I will leave out the *really bad* words and mention a few that you might not realize can get you into legal trouble.

Never refer to an employee as "crazy," "nuts," "wacko," "paranoid," or "schizoid," even if he or she is. Discrimination against an employee because of mental disability can sometimes land you in legal trouble; so can *harassment* because of mental disability (or physical disability). You can talk to your fellow managers about, or discipline or discharge an employee for, the employee's poor *job performance*, but do so using nondiagnostic language. Don't "diagnose" the employee yourself unless you are a psychiatrist. If you suspect that the employee is mentally unfit, you may have the right to ask the employee to submit to a mental examination.[49] You may, depending on how bad the employee's behavior or job performance is, have the right to terminate the employee without a mental examination. But don't play psychiatrist. If anyone is going to make a mental diagnosis, let it be a psychiatrist or other qualified mental health professional.

Never, ever, tell an employee that he or she is "too old." Don't even tell someone else that an employee is "too old." Don't say "old fart," "old fogey," "old geezer," "geezer," "dinosaur," or any other words meaning or implying old age. Don't say "We need younger people around here" or "We need new

---

49   Americans with Disabilities Act, 42 U.S.C. §12112(A). According to EEOC Policy Guidance: "The Americans with Disabilities Act and Psychiatric Disabilities" (March 25, 1997), "[M]edical examinations are permitted . . . if they address reasonable concerns about whether an individual is fit to perform essential functions of his/her position." Such examinations are particularly permitted when "an employer has a reasonable belief, based on objective evidence, that . . . an employee will pose a direct threat due to a medical condition." Retrieved from http://www.eeoc.gov/policy/docs/psych.html (last visited Mar. 14, 2013).

blood in this department." If you need personnel changes in a department, say "We need personnel changes in this department." You can terminate older employees just as you can terminate younger employees, but don't do it just *because* they are old, and certainly *don't tell them* they are old. Don't ever say "He's a good young marketing manager." An older worker will take offense at that, might make a note of it, and might use it against you someday in an age discrimination suit.

Don't refer to any racial, ethnic, or religious group as "you people." Don't say *"you women!"* or *"you men!"* In other words, don't lump people together just because they belong to a particular racial, ethnic, religious, or gender group. If a Jewish employee orders a ham sandwich for lunch, don't say, "I thought Jews don't eat pork." Some Jews do, others don't. Don't talk about an employee's religion unless the employee brings it up, in which case you should still try to politely stay away from the topic (except that you may need to discuss it if the employee is asking for some type of religious accommodation, such as leaving by 5:00 on Fridays, not working Sundays, etc.).

If you are a man, don't refer to a female over the age of 18 as a "girl." She is a "woman." Don't say "the girls in the office." Say "the women in the office" or, better yet, "the people in the office." Don't say "PMS," "that time of the month again," or any other words or phrases pertaining to menstruation.

If you are a woman, particularly a woman supervisor, don't say things that might lead a man to sue for sex discrimination. For example, don't say "It's their male culture" or "That's a guy thing" or "There's too much testosterone in this department."

If you work in one of the approximately seventeen states (or the District of Columbia) in which discrimination against gays, lesbians, and bisexuals is illegal, don't say any negative word about homosexuality. Don't talk about homosexuality at all in those states.

Language that is particularly offensive to members of a certain race, color, ethnicity, national origin, gender, religion, age (especially if over 40), physical or mental disability, or sexual orientation can get you into legal trouble. It can and will be used against you in court if an employee ever sues you for discrimination. It may even be the basis for the suit. It may be the only evidence the employee has. But it may be enough for the employee to win.

Have a Written Policy Prohibiting Discriminatory Slurs and Discriminatory Harassment, and Distribute It to All Employees

It is a good idea for employers to have a written policy distributed to employees that prohibits harassment, slurs, and other adverse behavior based on race, color, ethnicity, national origin, ancestry, sex, sexual orientation, pregnancy, age, religion, and disability. The policy will inform all your employees what type of behavior is unacceptable. Having such a policy might shield your company or organization from liability for *punitive* damages if your company or organization is ever held liable for discrimination or harassment.[50] In some cases, it might shield your company or organization from liability altogether.

Should you have a policy that bans *all* forms of harassment (a "No Harassment of Any Kind" policy), not just discriminatory or unlawful harassment? The problem with a "No Harassment of Any Kind" policy is that some employees feel "harassed" anytime the employer tries to get the employee to work harder or better. If an employee is constantly late to work, and you are constantly warning the employee that tardiness could lead the employee's dismissal, the employee might feel that you are "harassing" him or her, especially if, in the opinion of the employee, the employee feels that he or she has a good excuse for being late. To some employees, any effort by a supervisor to counsel an employee, warn an employee, or improve an employee's job performance is "harassment." Thus, the line between "harassment" and "supervision" is not always clear. Even if the counseling does not amount to "harassment," an employee might think it is harassment. Thus, having a "No Harassment of Any Kind" policy might make your managers afraid to discipline an employee. Managers might fear they will be accused of "harassing" the employee. Suffice it to say that supervisors should not engage in any type of *discriminatory* (or *illegal*) harassment. Also, some states are contemplating passing laws prohibiting any and all harassment or "bullying" in the workplace, so keep an eye on legislative developments regarding harassment and bullying.

---

50   See *Kolstad v. American Dental Association*, 527 U.S. 526 (1999); EEOC Enforcement Guidance: "Vicarious Employer Liability for Unlawful Harassment by Supervisors" (June 18, 1999).

Chapter Six

Some Tips to Reduce Damages and Lawyers' Fees

So much of human resources management these days is based on fear of lawsuits and fear of lawyers fees—if an employee sues a company, the company has to pay the company's lawyer or law firm to defend the company in the lawsuit, and if the employee wins the suit, the employer will also be required to pay the employee and might also be required to pay the employee's lawyer or law firm—that I want to offer some of my thoughts and tips on how employers can reduce such costs.

As an employer, you should try to keep your legal expenses low. But what do I mean by "legal expenses?" Do I just mean the money your company pays your company's lawyer or law firm? No, that is not all I mean. Heck, the money your company pays to your company's lawyer can possibly (but not necessarily) be kept low simply by hiring an inexpensive lawyer. Is that a good idea? Maybe, maybe not. It is possible that your company might save money on lawyer fees, but your company might (or, then again, might not) lose money in other ways if the inexpensive lawyer is not as knowledgeable or skillful as a more expensive lawyer.

So, should you hire a high-priced lawyer? Most high-priced lawyers are very good lawyers but they are also very good at making money. High-priced lawyers who represent employers make most of their money *from the employers.*

The employers (companies) pay substantial fees or salaries to their lawyers (fees to their outside law firms, salaries to their in-house lawyers if they have in-house lawyers). With *some* (not all, but *some*) high-priced lawyers, even if the lawyer's advice is good, the lawyer's fees are high to a point where the employer ends up with less money than if the employer had hired a lower-priced lawyer. It is also important to keep in mind that the "price" of legal services is sometimes difficult to measure. One reason is that a law firm that charges $500 per hour might be able to handle a case by doing 50 hours of work (total fee: $25,000), while a law firm that charges $300 per hour might do 100 hours of work (total fee: $30,000) to achieve the same result. Which is the more expensive firm? It is debatable. Of course, it is also possible that the law firm that charges $500 per hour will do 100 hours of work in the case (total fee: $50,000), while the $300-per-hour law firm might do 50 hours of work (total fee: $15,000) to achieve the same result. One problem with evaluating lawyer fees is that you never know what the result would have been had you hired a different lawyer. You don't know what the lawyer's fee would have been, and you don't know what the result of the case would have been.

In my view, a company's "legal expenses" in employment law consist of (approximately) eight items: 1) the money the company pays the lawyer or law firm who advises and represents the company in employment law; 2) the money the company pays, in the form of "damages," to employees (and in some cases, to the employees' lawyers) who sue the company or threaten to sue the company, 3) the money the company pays to employees in the form of severance packages in exchange for the employees' signing a waiver (sometimes called a "release") that waives (or "releases") their right to sue the company; 4) the money the company throws away in wages and salaries to employees that the company would like to fire but is afraid to fire due to the company's fear of lawsuits; 5) the money the company pays to human resources (HR) managers and other managers to document employee mistakes and poor job performance (one can argue that this documentation serves the purpose of trying to improve the employee's job performance, but in many companies the main reason they do all this documentation is to defend themselves if an employee sues the company or threatens to sue the company); 6) the lost productivity that results when employees, who think the company is afraid to fire them due to the company's fear of lawsuits, do not work as hard or as well as they are capable of working; 7) the money the company pays to the government in fines and other expenses if the company violates a labor law or employment law; and 8) if the company purchases employment practices liability insurance, the money the company spends to purchase that insurance. Maybe there are additional items I have not thought of, but those eight are the ones that come to my mind. With some law firms, the law firm is good at helping you keep one or more of these eight items low but you realize no savings from it because their advice to you causes the other items to be high. In my opinion, and this is just my opinion (perhaps others would disagree), the ideal law firm is the one that helps you keep the sum total of items (1), (2), (3), (4), (5), (6), (7), and (8) as low as possible. That is what I think law firms should try to do. Keeping the sum total of these eight items as low as possible should be the goal of law firms, employers, and society as a whole. Hopefully, the suggestions I have made in this book will help employers lower the sum total of those eight items.

I have one more suggestion. If you are an employer in Connecticut, Massachusetts, or one of the other states that has an employment discrimination law (a state law) that enables, or possibly enables, an employee to collect higher damages in an employment discrimination lawsuit than the federal laws do, you should consider doing this: Ask your state senator, state representative, and/or governor to put a maximum limit of $50,000 to $300,000, depending on how many employees your company or organization has, on the amount of money a court can force a company or organization to pay an employee for "emotional distress" and "punitive" damages in an employment discrimination lawsuit in your state. If your company has fewer than 15 employees, consider asking for a maximum limit on "emotional distress" and "punitive" damages *lower than* $50,000 (say, $20,000). Such maximum limits (called *caps*, or *damage caps*) exist under most of the *federal* employment discrimination laws,[51] but the federal employment discrimination laws allow each state, if a state so chooses, to "award" (force an employer to pay an employee) higher damages than the federal law allows. Under federal employment discrimination law, an employee who wins a discrimination lawsuit can collect from the employer the amount of money

---

51 See 42 U.S.C. § 1981a(b)(3), except that the cap does not apply in race discrimination cases. Again, to repeat what I said earlier, "U.S.C." in this book, and in most aspects of law, stands for United States Code, not University of Southern California. The United States Code is a compilation of federal statutes.

the employee lost as a result of the discrimination, plus an amount of money for emotional distress and punitive damages. Except in race discrimination lawsuits, where there is no cap on damages, the amount for emotional distress and punitive damages is capped at $50,000 if the employer has 15 to 100 employees, $100,000 if the employer has 101 to 200 employees, $200,000 if the employer has 201-500 employees, and $300,000 if the employer has more than 500 employees.

Massachusetts,[52] Connecticut,[53] and some other states have no caps. Suppose a very small employer in Massachusetts, say, an employer with only 8 employees, decides to terminate an employee. Let's say the employee was making $12 per hour ($24,000 per year). If the employee sues for discrimination, and a jury decides the employer should be compelled to pay the employee five million dollars, the employer might have to pay the employee five million dollars. If the employer doesn't have five million dollars, the employer might have to declare bankruptcy. By contrast, a small employer (8 employees) in a state that has damage caps (as described in the above paragraph) would have to pay as follows. Let us assume that the employee is out of work for one year after being fired, then lands another job paying $12 per hour. The employer would have to pay the employee $24,000 (the amount of money the employee lost as a result of the discrimination), plus a maximum of (no more than) $20,000 for emotional distress. That is a total—and maximum—of $44,000. Plus, the employer would have to pay the employee's lawyer's fees. So, with damage caps, the maximum total is probably (there may be an occasional exception to this) between $60,000 and $80,000. Without damage caps, the sky is the limit. If the jury says the employer should pay the employee five million dollars, the employer might have to pay the employee five million dollars. This, in my opinion, is one reason employers leave Connecticut and Massachusetts or don't enter Connecticut and Massachusetts to begin with. If an employer hires someone in Connecticut or Massachusetts, and then for some reason fires that employee, the employee can, with a good lawyer and a sympathetic jury, possibly bankrupt the employer. In states with damage caps, the damages more accurately reflect the economics of the business: A small employer would not have to pay a huge sum of money.

---

52   Mass. General Laws chapter 151B, § 9.

53   Conn. General Statutes § 46a-104.

Putting a cap on damages would almost certainly reduce the number of employment discrimination lawsuits. Why? Because many employees would not sue if the most they could collect were $50,000 (or even $100,000, $200,000, or $300,000) plus their lost wages and attorney's fees. Many sue only if they have a chance of winning millions or many hundreds of thousands of dollars. They sue the way they buy lottery tickets: They don't buy a ticket if the prize is "only" $50,000 but will wait in line all day and buy 20 tickets when the prize is $50 million. The odds against winning $50 million are astronomical, and nearly everyone could benefit from winning "only" $50,000, yet they don't enter the "game" if the prize is "only" $50,000. These people enter only if they can win millions or many hundreds of thousands of dollars. Many employees who sue employers think that way. They have a lottery mentality.

Damages in defamation suits and some other types of employee lawsuits would still have no cap in many states. Maybe your state legislature would be willing to impose caps in all employee lawsuits, but I don't know.

If these states, including Massachusetts and Connecticut, were to impose this cap on emotional distress damages and punitive damages in employment discrimination lawsuits, employers in these states would no longer have to worry that a court might order them to pay millions of dollars in emotional distress damages and/or punitive damages in such a lawsuit. Even if a jury were to "award" such a large amount, the judge would be required by law to reduce the emotional-distress and punitive components of the "award" to $300,000 if the employer has 500 or more employees, $200,000 if the employer has 201-500 employees, $100,000 if the employer has 101-200 employees, $50,000 if the employer has 15-100 employees, and less than $50,000 if the employer has fewer than 15 employees.

Because the potential damages in these cases would be considerably lower, settlement amounts would be considerably lower too. Why settle a case for $500,000 if the most you can lose at trial is $200,000? Likewise, lawyer fees would be lower. A law firm will have difficulty charging an employer $100,000 to defend against an employment discrimination lawsuit if the most the employer can lose in the lawsuit is $50,000. Also, employers feel compelled to spend far more for "preventive" legal services if damages are uncapped than if damages are capped.

Outrageously high jury verdicts are rare, but they can happen in any case, and thus have the effect of scaring employers in many states (such as Massachusetts and Connecticut) into thinking they must spend vast sums of money to settle cases and prevent future cases. Many employers decide that the best way to prevent future cases is to not hire at all, or move out of Massachusetts or Connecticut and into a state that has damage caps.

Another way to address this problem (the problem of uncapped damages for emotional distress and punitive damages in Connecticut, Massachusetts, and some other states) is to ask Congress to pass a law declaring that no state's employment discrimination law can provide higher damage awards than are allowed under the analogous federal law. Whether Congress would be willing to pass such a law, I don't know. You may want to write to your Congressperson, U.S. Senator, and/or the President about this.

I am not a lobbyist. I am just trying to help employers reduce their costs. Over the past 35 years, I have seen employers in Connecticut, Massachusetts, and some other states spend huge sums of money on lawyers, trainers, and human resources (HR) consultants due to the employers' enormous fear of employment lawsuits. This enormous fear drives many HR decisions. Many employees are allowed to be mediocre and unproductive because their bosses are afraid to fire them, due to the potential cost of such a lawsuit. This book hopefully will help employers reduce the number of, and cost of, these lawsuits. One way this book does so is by teaching employers how to prevent discrimination in the first place. Another way is to point out to employers that they can try to get their lawmakers to put a cap on emotional-distress damages and punitive damages in state-law employment discrimination lawsuits.

If someone tells you that a cap on damages in employment discrimination lawsuits would be unconstitutional or invalid in any way, ask them the basis of their assertion. Ask them exactly why they think such a cap would be unconstitutional or invalid. What section of state law, the state constitution, federal law, or the federal (U.S.) Constitution would be violated? Courts in some states have held caps on damages in personal injury lawsuits (lawsuits in which someone was physically injured) unconstitutional because personal injury law is, for the most part, a "common law tort" which has traditionally been decided, as to liability and damages, by juries, but I am not aware of any courts holding caps on damages in employment discrimination lawsuits unconstitutional. Employment discrimination lawsuits are statutory (not "common law"), so legislatures have the authority to put limits on them.

Conclusion

When the Only Color Is Green

Discrimination is illegal, immoral, abusive, and should end. Employers should not discriminate on the basis of race, color, gender, age, national origin, religion, disability, or genetics. In states that prohibit discrimination on the basis of sexual orientation, employers should not discriminate on that basis, either. Personally, I believe that employers should not discriminate on the basis of sexual orientation even if such discrimination is legal in their state, but that topic is complicated and controversial in many states, so I will leave it at that rather than take a political stand.

Employers should not stereotype their employees. Employers should not make assumptions about men, women, whites, blacks, Latinos, Asians, Muslims, older workers, gays, and disabled workers based on what *some* men, women, whites, blacks, Latinos, Asians, Muslims, older workers, gays, and disabled workers do. Employers should not lump people together just because they are the same race, color, national origin, gender, religion, age, sexual orientation, or have the same disability. Employers should treat each person as an *individual* who may be very different from others of his or her race, color, national origin, gender, religion, age, sexual orientation, or disability group.

But some employers will continue to discriminate anyway. It is difficult to "cure" them of it because they don't think they are "sick." Many employers who discriminate do not even realize they discriminate. They claim, and they honestly believe, that the only "color" they see is "green"—money. They claim that all their decisions are based on "the bottom line." If they fire someone, they claim it is because firing that person will somehow improve "the bottom line." "I don't care if an employee is black, white, brown, red, blue, male, female, young, or old," they claim. "All I care about is how well they perform." That is what employers tell judges and juries when employers go to court to defend against discrimination lawsuits. Many of these employers are lying. But many others are telling the truth. It is difficult to know who is lying and who is telling the truth. That is why so many employ*ees* lose these suits. The burden of proof in court is usually on the plaintiff, not the defendant. The plaintiff in an employment discrimination suit is the employ*ee*, not the employ*er*. If the employee cannot prove the employer is lying, the employee usually loses.

Years ago it was easier for employees to win these suits. Employers made more racist, sexist, and "ageist" (pertaining to old age) remarks back then. "We don't hire blacks." "A woman can't do this job." "You're too old for this job." "Irish need not apply." Employers would make these remarks, and these remarks would be used against them in court to prove discrimination. Those employers would lose in court.

But few employers make such remarks today. Employers who discriminate against blacks, women, and older workers today usually do so quietly. Discrimination is more subtle today. It is harder to prove discrimination today.

Thus, not only is it difficult to "cure" employers who discriminate today, it is difficult to "catch" them and bring them to justice.

As I said, however, many employers who claim their decisions are based on "the bottom line" rather than on discriminatory factors really are telling the truth. According to syndicated career-advice columnist Joyce Lain Kennedy, most layoff decisions are based on "who earns their keep and who doesn't." "The key determinant of who survives layoffs is each employee's input to profit potential, based on his or her previous impact on bottom-line issues," she says.[54] Occasionally a layoff decision is based on gender, age, race, or other discriminatory factors, she says, but most are based on "who earns their keep and who doesn't."

---

54   Joyce Lain Kennedy, "Why Was Model Employee Laid Off?" *Springfield* (Mass.) *Sunday Republican*, June 10, 2001, p. E4, quoting Paul Hawkinson, *The Fordyce Letter* (an employment newsletter).

A layoff decision based on "who earns their keep and who doesn't" is legally, ethically, and morally acceptable. It is difficult to criticize employers for basing decisions on "the bottom line." The bottom line should not be their *only* consideration, of course. Employers should also consider the economic and ecological effects of their operations and the good of all persons involved. But basing decisions on the bottom line is good in this sense: It means, hopefully, that the employer is not basing decisions on race, gender, age, or other discriminatory factors.

Although it is true that some employers who think they don't discriminate really do discriminate, it is also true that some employees who think they are *victims* of discrimination really are not. Many employees (and many other types of people) tend to blame their problems on "circumstances beyond their control," such as their race, gender, or age. "I got fired. It must be because of my age." "My boss doesn't like me. It must be because I'm a woman." "I'm eighty pounds overweight. It must be that I have a low metabolism or a genetic predisposition toward being fat." "I'm an alcoholic. It must be because my father drank a lot." Some of these people are correct, but others are not. Others assume their problems are due to their gender, age, race, or other "circumstances beyond their control," but they are mistaken. Their problems are really due to their *inability, bad habits, lack of self-discipline,* and *difficult personalities.* These people can change and improve if they really try to, but they don't really try to. They accept little or no responsibility for their own predicaments. They don't try to correct their own faults. They blame others. Or they blame "circumstances beyond their control," such as their race, gender, or age. An employee who does not get along with her boss might blame it on the boss's being of a different race, gender, or age than she is. Those are "circumstances beyond her control." But in fact, the problem might be *her own* attitude, inability, poor work habits, or lack of self-discipline. Those are circumstances *within* her control.

Of course, it is also possible that the problem really is the boss's fault and not her fault. But that does not necessarily mean the boss is discriminating. It may mean that the boss has some problem himself—personality, attitude, stupidity, or whatever— but not in regard to race, gender, or age. So a discrimination lawsuit will not end the problem.

This phenomenon—blaming circumstances *beyond* one's control rather than factors *within* one's control—is exemplified by the job hunter who has a pimple on his forehead. He goes on three interviews but no one hires him. No one tells him why he is not hired, but he assumes it is because he looks a little funny with a pimple on his forehead. That is not necessarily the reason, though. The real reason may be that he didn't interview well or he interviewed well but not as well as the successful applicant did, or his résumé wasn't quite as good as the successful applicant's. He really doesn't know. Maybe he should try to get rid of the pimple, but he shouldn't dwell too much on the pimple. He should try to improve his résumé and interview skills, and not draw conclusions after only three interviews. Maybe the pimple had something to do with it, maybe it didn't. Maybe the pimple had something to do with one job rejection but not the other two.

He might also wish to ask one of the interviewers why he didn't get the job. It is possible the interviewer will not tell him the reason, but it is also possible the interviewer will tell him the reason. The rejected applicant will never know unless he asks. This is also true of an employee who gets fired or is about to be fired. Rather than assume it is because of race, age, gender, or handicap, he or she might wish to speak to the boss and ask the boss what the problem is. Making assumptions rather than speaking face to face with the boss is like choosing darkness over light. Speaking to the boss will not necessarily yield the entire truth, for maybe the boss really is discriminating on the basis of race, age, gender, or handicap—and will try to hide the truth. But maybe some light will come from the conversation. There is at least some chance that the employee will learn to see herself as others see her.

Knowing oneself as one is known by others is a key to career success. People who feel they were fired or not hired because of their race, gender, age, or other discriminatory reason should be open to the possibility that that was *not* the reason. Maybe it was, maybe it wasn't. As we noted, years ago many employees did not have to *wonder* whether they were victims of discrimination. They knew they were victims of discrimination. They would apply for a job and be told, "No Negroes." A pregnant woman would get fired from a job and be told, "A pregnant woman can't do this job." But as we noted, those days are largely gone. Few employers say those things today. Today a black employee who gets fired after fifteen years on the job and feels he is a victim of race discrimination might have difficulty proving that race had anything to do with the firing. His boss probably did not make a racist remark or otherwise display prejudice against blacks. The boss will defend against the suit by saying, "You were black when I hired you. You were black the entire fifteen years you worked here. If I were prejudiced against blacks,

I would not have hired you. Or I would have fired you a long time ago. So obviously I am not prejudiced against blacks. I fired you for reasons other than your race, namely, your poor job performance and poor attitude. You should try to improve your job performance and attitude." As blunt and simplistic as the boss sounds, he may be telling the truth. The employee's job performance and attitude really may have been poor. It may be that a white employee with the same poor job performance and attitude would have been fired, too. If a white employee with the same poor job performance and attitude would have been fired, there was no discrimination. The black employee was treated exactly the way the white employee would have been.

That is why it is often difficult for an employee who worked for an employer for many years to sue the employer for race discrimination, gender discrimination, religion discrimination, or national origin discrimination. The employer hired that employee and kept that employee on the payroll for many years even though that employee was of that race, gender, religion, and national origin. It is difficult to accuse the employer of suddenly discriminating against that employee due to race, gender, religion, or national origin.

That is the sad irony of employment discrimination law. Most of the suits are initiated by people who were fired, not by rejected job applicants. Yet the people who were fired usually aren't the ones who were discriminated against, so most of them either lose or receive very little money in the suit. The rejected job applicants—the people who weren't hired to begin with— are more likely to be the ones who were discriminated against. Yet they rarely sue. We discussed this in chapter 5 ("The Story of the Latino Factory Worker"). Whatever the reason for this irony, it teaches us that preventing discrimination in the workplace requires effort by employers *and* employees. Just suing, threatening, lecturing, and cajoling the employers won't end it.

The most important "color" in the workplace is not black or white. It is "green." "Green" can mean *money*, or it can mean *environmentally friendly*. Either way, "green" is the most important color in the workplace. Your decisions should be based on the economic, and hopefully also the ecological, "bottom line," not on an employee's skin color, gender, age, ethnicity, or other discriminatory category. You shouldn't care if an employee is black, white, brown, red, or some other color. You should care how well they perform their job.

Perhaps the best tip we can give employ*ees* to prevent discrimination in the workplace is to be the best employee you can be. The best employees are discriminated against far less than the mediocre employees are. Most employers don't want to do anything to offend or lose the best employees. They want to keep the best employees. Most employers really do care more about "green" than any other color.

So it all boils down to this: Employers should not discriminate, but at the same time, employees should not be too quick to accuse employers of discrimination.

Index

in the private sector, on average, lawsuits are brought by fired or laid-off employees more often than by employees who are still employed by the employer or who were never hired by the employer to begin with, 47, 87

Lawyers, 1, 3, 4, 8, 10, 21, 44, 47, 71-72, 77-82

Lobbying, 13, 26, 67, 79-82

Marceau, Marcel (pantomime artist), 23

Marriage, 64

Maternity leave, 37-40, 58

Multiculturalism, 11-12, 22-23

National origin discrimination (see Race discrimination)

Obama, Barack, ix, 42, 69-70

Peter, Laurence J., Dr. (on racism), 11

Policy, company or organization (see Written policy)

Posters, displaying required, 70

Pregnancy,
    disability (pregnancy usually is not regarded as a "disability" under federal disability discrimination law), 38, 58
    Family and Medical Leave Act (FMLA), 38
    maternity leave, 37-40, 58
    should be treated like any short-term illness, 37
    why employers should not discriminate against pregnant women (besides fact that such

discrimination is usually illegal), 38-39

"Protected classifications" (use and misuse of term), 6-7, 36

Puerto Ricans (see also Latinos), 23

Quinn, Jane Bryant (on women's income and how it affects their husbands' housework), 39

Race discrimination,
    "accentuate the negative" (employers should not do this), 16-18
    "color-blind" is what employers should try to be, 11-18, 21, 26-27, 49
    eliminating racial slurs, 71-74
    intellect is unrelated to skin-color, 16, 32
    interchangeability of words "race" and "color," 6, 12
    Slavery, 24
    stereotyping (see Stereotyping)

REGARDS (acronym for Race, Ethnicity, Gender, Age, Religion, Disability, and Sexual orientation), 2, 5-6

Religion discrimination, 50-52

"Retaliation" (discrimination against an employee because the employee complained about discrimination), 42

Reverse discrimination (see Discrimination, reverse)

Ricci v. DeStephano (U.S. Supreme Court case involving New Haven firefighters), 11, 19

Romney, Mitt, 22-23

SATs and IQ tests, 16, 32

About the Author

David A. Robinson is a professor (his title is practitioner-in-residence) at the University of New Haven in West Haven, Connecticut, and a labor lawyer. In his labor law practice, he usually represents employ*ers*, but he occasionally has represented employ*ees*. He practiced law in Springfield, Massachusetts, from 1977 to 2008, and now practices in Connecticut. He is a member of the Connecticut Bar and a retired member of the Massachusetts Bar. He received a bachelor's degree in economics from George Washington University in 1974 and a law degree from Washington University in St. Louis in 1977. At U. of New Haven, he has taught human resource management, business law, business ethics, criminal justice, and the law of communications.

Made in the USA
Lexington, KY
13 April 2014